The 2025 Jubilee in Rome

The Complete Pilgrim Guide

The 2025 Jubilee in Rome

The Complete Pilgrim Guide

Bret Thoman, OFS

Icona Press
Peachtree City, Georgia

ICONA PRESS

This book is dedicated to all pilgrims who will journey to Rome this year. May they be blessed abundantly.

Contents

And so I say to you, you are Peter, and upon this rock I will build my church, and the gates of the netherworld shall not prevail against it.

(Matthew 16:18)

Preface

I came to Rome the first time when I was nineteen years old. I was a college student enrolled in a language course in Florence. Having never been out of the United States, I was captivated by the eternal city. I was stunned by the vast richness of history, art and architecture, and cultural sites. The modern hustle and bustle superimposed over so many ancient ruins seemed harmonious in an odd sort of way. In fact, I found the utter chaos of Rome charming. But what struck me most about Rome were the churches and long Christian history.

At that point in my life, I was Protestant. As a child, I had been baptized and confirmed as a Lutheran, though I was attending a non-denominational church then. I believed in Jesus Christ, but I was still trying to sort it all out. I struggled to reconcile so many contradictory beliefs and denominations that abounded in my home country.

My impression of Rome was quite different from Martin Luther's when he visited the eternal city as an Augustinian friar and priest in 1510 or so. He went away disillusioned with the worldliness of the clergy and prelates, and just a few years later, he codified his criticisms of the Roman Church in his famous 95 theses. I, on the other hand, was inspired by the rich beauty and splendor of it all. Moreover, I could not avoid one inescapable conclusion: the Catholic Church traced its roots to the apostles Peter and Paul, whose tombs were safeguarded by magnificent basilicas. It was clear that the Catholic Church had an unbroken line directly to those two apostles, in particular Peter. Not long after that summer, I enrolled in RCIA and was confirmed fully into the Catholic Church.

A journey to Rome during a Jubilee Year is the experience of a lifetime. It allows visitors to experience firsthand the Holy See of St. Peter. Pilgrims can enter into the history of the Church—from its earliest years—by walking in the footsteps of the first apostles and disciples. Rome's awe and grandeur will not disappoint.

As Rome had such an impact on my personal and spiritual life, it is my hope that the city of St. Peter will leave a lasting impact on all who read this book.

May the intercession of Saints Peter and Paul guide you as you begin your journey.

Part I: The 2025 Jubilee

Introduction to Pilgrimage

L ife is a journey, a pilgrimage. The word derives from the Latin word *peregrinare*, meaning "to wander through fields." Pilgrimage seems to be innate to the human experience, almost as an archetype. Sacred journeys or quests are present in mythological literature, and pilgrimages are part of many religious traditions.

The Bible is filled with many vocation narratives, that is, when God calls a person or groups of people to leave one place for another. The first biblical "pilgrimage" is recounted in Genesis, when Abram was called by Yahweh to leave his father's home and pagan past and set out to a land where he would receive divine blessings (see Genesis 12:1-4). Then, under the leadership of Moses, the Israelites come out of Egypt and make their way to Mount Sinai (see Exodus 19).

In these narratives, Abraham and Moses follow the voice of God, who leads them on a journey, at the end of which he gives them covenants. Abram leaves pagan Haran for Canaan, where he receives a new name, Abraham. Moses leaves Egypt, where the Israelites were enslaved by Pharaoh, for Mount Sinai, where God gives him the law. In both cases, the journey involved a period of struggle, which involved uncertainty, hardship, and feelings of bewilderment and confusion. Yet, they ultimately arrived at a better place. They hear the call of God and leave, wander, and ultimately arrive purified and in a better state.

In the New Testament, the theme of pilgrimage continues. However, the journey involving departure, exile, and arrival is embodied in the Word, that is, Christ. The "journey" of Christ can be summarized in the Nicene Creed:

> For us men and our salvation He came down from heaven: by the power of the Holy Spirit, He was born of the Virgin Mary, and became man. For our sake He was crucified under Pontius Pilate; He suffered, died, and was buried. On the third day He rose again in fulfillment

of the scriptures: He ascended into heaven and is seated at the right hand of the Father.

Jesus, whose "kingdom was not of this world" (see John 18:36), obeyed his Father, left his "homeland" in Heaven, and became incarnate as a man in the world. In his worldly life as a "sojourner," he, too, experienced suffering and exile and felt like a stranger. As Abraham and Moses "wandered" through the desert, Jesus "had nowhere to rest his head" (Luke 9:58). Finally, like the prophets, Jesus ultimately went to a better place after his Resurrection. Unlike them, however, Heaven was the place he had originally left. Thus, his pilgrimage took him full circle from his Father's house in Heaven through the "insecurity" of earth and back to Heaven.

Like Jesus and the prophets, Christ's followers are called to a similar trajectory. Scripture calls Christians to become "strangers and aliens on earth" (Hebrews 11:14). Peter exhorted his followers "as aliens and sojourners to keep away from worldly desires that wage war against the soul" (1 Peter 2:11) and to "conduct yourselves with reverence during the time of your sojourning" (1 Peter 1:17). In this sense, the state of exile is not the Christian's ultimate goal; Heaven is. The Christian vocation is transcendent. The journey requires the purification of the soul toward holiness while passing through the brokenness of the world in order to arrive at a future paradise.

Beginning in the late classical and early medieval periods, pilgrimage was seen in the monastic tradition as an interior journey of the soul. St. Augustine of Hippo (354-430) believed that Christians should live a life of peregrination (pilgrimage) in the present world while awaiting the Kingdom of God. He wrote, "There remains after baptism the crossing of the desert, by a life that is lived in hope, until we come to the promised land, to the land of the living where God is our portion, to the eternal Jerusalem; until we get there, the whole of this life is the desert for us, the whole of it a trial and temptation."

If the Christian pilgrimage was initially considered a metaphor for the purgative journey of the soul, it would also be expressed as the traditional geographical journey. After Emperor Constantine legalized Christianity in the Edict of Milan in 313, he set out to promote the formerly banned religion by building large basilicas in Rome over the tombs of Sts. Peter and Paul, as well as other basilicas in honor of St. Mary and St. John. Meanwhile, his mother, Helena, went on a pilgrimage to the Holy Land, where she, too, erected churches and shrines to memorialize events from the Gospels. She also brought back relics to Rome, sparking interest in the holy places related to Jesus' earthly life. These large churches and events paved the way, so to speak, for Christians to come. With that, Christians began journeying to the Holy Land. The important sites were in Nazareth, where the Annunciation took place; Bethlehem, where Jesus was born; and Jerusalem, where Christ suffered, died, and rose from the dead.

By the eleventh century, the practice of pilgrimage had become widespread and more thoroughly integrated into Christian devotion. Much was owed to the Crusades. The stories told by the crusaders after returning home stirred the desire to go to the sacred places of Jesus' life. The desire to go on pilgrimage was so strong that Christians risked disease, violence, shipwrecks, and strife. Many did not return home. Before setting off, they prepared a last will and testament, gave away or sold their possessions, and celebrated a pilgrimage liturgical rite similar to that of a funeral. After donning the characteristic garb, the pilgrim left. The pilgrim's dress set them apart and identified them as such. It consisted of a tunic with an in-sewn cross, a walking staff, and a leather pouch to carry food and money. A broad-brimmed hat was often worn with a long scarf wrapped around the body from the back to the waist. Certain symbols were also displayed. The scallop shell was used on the tunics of those headed to Compostela, while the keys were worn by those going to Rome.

While the Holy Land was considered the queen of all pilgrimages, Christians also went to Rome to visit the tombs of Sts. Peter and Paul and the early martyrs, to Compostela in Spain to visit the tomb of St. James, and to Monte Sant'Angelo to visit the grotto where St. Michael appeared. At the same time, there were countless local shrines and sanctuaries on the outskirts of villages and towns. These offered Christians of little means the opportunity to go on pilgrimage as well as a place to go that was safe.

During this period, pilgrimage was considered a penitential act. Sometimes, one's confessor would prescribe a pilgrimage as a penance after confession. Other times, the faithful set out on pilgrimage to receive indulgences. According to Catholic teaching, an indulgence is the full or partial remission of temporal punishment for sins after confession and absolution. In 1300 A.D., Pope Boniface instituted the first Jubilee Year, granting a plenary indulgence—that is, the full remission of punishment—to pilgrims who journeyed to Rome. Other pilgrimages, such as to the Holy Land, could also grant the plenary indulgence.

Other reasons for going on pilgrimage were to connect with particular saints to whom one had a strong devotion. Over the centuries, shrines and sanctuaries were built to mark places associated with the life of a saint: the site of their birthplace, martyrdom, or death; where mystical events took place; or to their tombs. Other sanctuaries were known for miraculous healings and graces.

From the sixteenth century onward, the devotional practice of pilgrimage fell into decline. It virtually came to a halt in the Protestant countries as reformers challenged the theology of indulgences and sought to end every Christian devotion not explicitly taught in the Bible. During the Enlightenment, pilgrimages became even more obsolete as modern people began to look down on the devotion as archaic, irrational, or downright superstitious. At the same time, the modern concept of tourism was born in the form of the classical Grand Tour. Lasting several months, the sought-after voyage to the classical countries, mainly Italy, was the capstone of the education of young men from well-to-do families from northern Europe.

In recent times, the perennial value of pilgrimage has been rediscovered. More and more, contemporary people are seeking an authentic travel experience that leads to something more fulfilling (and transcendent) than tourism. Certainly, the conditions and motivations of pilgrimages are different from times past. While few pilgrims today are concerned with receiving a plenary indulgence, today's pilgrims have a powerful desire to silence the noise and leave behind the multitudinous vacuous distractions of modern life in order to discover places imbued with authenticity and truth. Moreover, jet airplanes, touring coaches, and all-inclusive hotels have rendered the journey less penitential. Nonetheless, jet lag, COVID swabs, and maintenance delays still require patience (and penance), leading to, hopefully, spiritual growth.

While the circumstances are different, the essence of pilgrimage remains unchanged. It requires taking leave of the familiar for the unknown on a journey informed by faith. Pilgrimage begins with rupture when the pilgrim leaves home. After traveling to a foreign place, he becomes, in the biblical sense, a "pilgrim and stranger." Eventually, at some point along the journey, the feeling of being a foreigner subsides, and the inner sense of familiarity returns. In this process of departure, wandering, and arrival, the pilgrim becomes something he was not. He has experienced new places and met new people. He has listened to stories and witnessed places where extraordinary events took place. In the biblical sense, he has left the "old man" behind and been transformed. He has encountered the living God.

In his autobiographical tome, *The Seven Storey Mountain*, Thomas Merton captures the essence of pilgrimage:

In one sense, we are always traveling, and traveling as if we did not know where we were going. In another sense, we have already arrived. We cannot arrive at the perfect possession of God in this life, and that is why we are traveling and in darkness. But we already possess Him by grace, and therefore, in that sense, we have arrived and are dwelling in the light. But oh! How far have I to go to find You in Whom I have already arrived! (New York: New American Library, 1948, p. 409)

The *Catechism of the Catholic Church* says that "Pilgrimages evoke our earthly journey toward heaven and are traditionally very special occasions for renewal in prayer. For pilgrims seeking living water, shrines are special places for living the forms of Christian prayer 'in Church.'" (2691). May God bless you as you begin your journey.

The Jubilee and Holy Door

The Jubilee

A Jubilee is a special year in which Catholics seek grace and holiness. It is marked by the remission of sins and pardon. The name derives from the instrument used to mark its launch—the *yobel*, or ram's horn, used to proclaim the Day of Atonement (Yom Kippur) by the Jewish people of old. Today, the Jewish people celebrate the feast every year, though in the Bible, a Jubilee was to be observed every fifty years.

> You shall count seven weeks of years—seven times seven years—such that the seven weeks of years amount to forty-nine years. Then, on the tenth day of the seventh month let the ram's horn resound; on this, the Day of Atonement, the ram's horn blast shall resound throughout your land. You shall treat this fiftieth year as sacred. You shall proclaim liberty in the land for all its inhabitants. It shall be a jubilee for you, when each of you shall return to your own property, each of you to your own family. This fiftieth year is your year of jubilee; you shall not sow, nor shall you reap the aftergrowth or pick the untrimmed vines, since this is the jubilee. It shall be sacred for you. You may only eat what the field yields of itself. (Leviticus 25:8-13)

In the Gospel of Luke, Jesus makes clear his own mission to bring Jubilee. In the synagogue at Nazareth, he reads from the scroll of the prophet Isaiah, proclaiming a year of the Lord's favor. Then he speaks.

> "The Spirit of the Lord is upon me, because he has anointed me to bring glad tidings to the poor. He has sent me to proclaim liberty to captives and recovery of sight to the blind, to let the oppressed go free, and to

proclaim a year acceptable to the Lord... Today this scripture passage is fulfilled in your hearing." (4:18-19; 21)

Thus, a Jubilee is an occasion to make reparation for sin and to renew one's commitment to conversion of life. It is an invitation to return to a right relationship with God, with one another, and with all of creation.

Jubilees in Rome began when Pope Boniface VIII called for the first "Holy Year" in 1300 A.D., granting a plenary indulgence to all pilgrims who visited the major basilicas of Rome during that year. He intended future Jubilees to be observed every century, though the frequency has changed over the centuries. In 1343, Pope Clement VI established that Holy Years be observed every fifty years. In 1470, Pope Paul II extended the inter-jubilee period to twenty-five years. In the twentieth century, "extraordinary" Jubilees were introduced within the 25-year cycle in order that everyone could experience a Holy Year. Pope Pius XI declared a Jubilee in 1933 to mark the 19th centenary of the death of Jesus Christ. Most recently, the Extraordinary Jubilee of Mercy was observed in 2016, during the pontificate of Pope Francis.

The Holy Door

Crossing the Holy Door is one of the most poignant moments during a Jubilee pilgrimage to Rome. The Holy Door, or *Porta Sancta*, represents a spiritual gateway, as it symbolizes crossing the threshold from sin to redemption.

In the Jewish tradition, only the high priest could enter the Holy of Holies. Once a year, on the Feast of Yom Kippur, the high priest would cross the veiled doorway of the Holy of Holies to enter into the presence of God and offer atonement for the sins of the Jewish people. It recalls Scripture: "This is the LORD's own gate, through it the righteous enter" (Psalm 118:20).

Christ fulfilled this Scripture when he said, "I am the gate. Whoever enters through me will be saved, and will come in and go out and find pasture" (John 10:9). He was declaring that anyone who wished to draw close to the Father must go through him. Once passed, the person will be blessed abundantly. The door, which symbolizes communion with God, is always open.

The Holy Door symbolizes the separation between the world and Heaven. Passing through the Holy Door of Rome's Major Basilicas represents the passage from this world into the presence of God. Crossing the threshold of the Holy Door is, thus, a statement of purpose, as it is connected to the other spiritual practices associated with the Jubilee, such as pilgrimage, reconciliation, personal and liturgical prayer, reception of the Eucharist, and profession of faith. In other words, it represents the intention to amend one's life. It represents metanoia. This is what Pope John Paul II announced to the world on the day of his election: "Open wide the doors to Christ."

The tradition of the Holy Door in Rome during a Jubilee dates to 1423, when Pope Martin V opened the Holy Door of the Basilica of Saint John Lateran for the first time. His successors maintained this tradition during Jubilees and extended it to the other major basilicas. In 1500, Pope Alexander VI formalized the tradition when he ordered that a special door in St. Peter's Basilica be bricked up and only opened during Jubilee years. Traditionally, the pope would use a hammer to strike the wall sealing the door, symbolically breaking the barrier between sin and grace. Upon the conclusion of the Holy Year, the door was once again bricked up. Today, for safety reasons, the bricks are dismantled several days before the ceremony, and the pope uses a key to open the door.

It is the Lord who says, "Behold, I stand at the door and knock. If anyone hears my voice and opens the door, [then] I will enter his house and dine with him, and he with me" (Revelation 3:20). A Jubilee is a time to open our hearts to him and cross the threshold of hope, striving for holiness.

Jubilee 2025: "Pilgrims of Hope"

For more information, visit the official Jubilee website:
www.iubilaeum2025.va/en.html

The Theme

The theme of the Jubilee in 2025 is "Pilgrims of Hope." Pope Francis has invited the faithful to renew our hope and discover a vision that can "restore access to the fruits of the earth to everyone." It is a call for all people to embark on a journey of spiritual renewal and reconciliation, to reflect on the past, embrace the present, and look forward to a future filled with hope.

The 2025 Jubilee Year begins on Christmas Eve 2024 and concludes on January 6, 2026. Holidays are expected to be the busiest, including Easter, All Saints, and Christmas. As for accommodation, it is advised is to book well in advance, at least three or four months for families or even close to a year for larger groups.

Throughout the year, there will be a number of important events, in which Pope Francis will be present:

- January 24-26: The Jubilee of Communication
- February 8-9: Jubilee of the Armed Forces
- February 15-18: the Jubilee of Artists
- March 8-9: the Jubilee of Volunteers
- April 5-6: the Jubilee of the sick and health care workers
- April 25-27: the Jubilee of adolescents/teenagers
- April 28-29: the Jubilee of people with disabilities
- May 1-4: the Jubilee of workers
- May 4-5: the Jubilee of entrepreneurs
- May 30-June 1: the Jubilee of families, including children, grandparents, and the elderly

- June 7-8: the Jubilee of movements, associations, and new communities
- June 9: the Jubilee of the Holy See
- June 14-15: the Jubilee of sports
- June 20-22: the Jubilee of government officials
- June 25: the Jubilee of bishops
- June 25-27: the Jubilee of priests
- July 28-August 3: the Jubilee of young people
- September 20: the Jubilee of justice workers
- October 4-5: the Jubilee of migrants
- October 31-November 2: the Jubilee of educators
- November 16: the Jubilee of the poor
- December 14: the Jubilee of prisoners.

The Pilgrim's Card

The Pilgrim's Card is a digital pass bearing the name of the holder, which will be necessary to participate in the main Jubilee events and to organize a pilgrimage to pass through the Holy Door. The Pilgrim's Card can be obtained at the following site: www.iubilaeum2025.va/en/carta-del-pellegrino

The card can only be obtained by signing up at the official portal, at
www.register.iubilaeum2025.va/user.
Otherwise, it can be obtained via the official Jubilee App for smartphones. After entering the required details, the pilgrim will receive a unique QR code and a personalized account on the app.

After signing up for the pilgrim's card and accessing one's personal account via the website or app, pilgrims will be able to sign up for their pilgrimage to the Holy Door of Saint Peter's Basilica and all the other main events of the Jubilee. This will allow orderly access both to the Holy Door and to the main

Jubilee events, at which large numbers of pilgrims are expected to be in attendance. The portal allows individuals or groups to register for events and note any disabilities or special access requirements. It also allows pilgrims to modify or cancel bookings, as well as manage the time, day, and month of their pilgrimage.

The Papal Bull of Indiction

According to tradition, each Jubilee is proclaimed through the publication of a "Bull of Indiction." A Papal Bull is a formal papal document bearing the papal seal (bulla, in Latin). The seal is a symbol of the pope's authority and is used to authenticate the document. Traditionally, bulls were written on parchment and sealed with a lead seal.

(Given in Rome, at Saint John Lateran, on 9 May, the Solemnity of the Ascension of our Lord Jesus Christ, in the year 2024, the twelfth of my Pontificate.)
Pope Francis

SPES NON CONFUNDIT
BULL OF INDICTION
OF THE ORDINARY JUBILEE
OF THE YEAR 2025
FRANCIS
BISHOP OF ROME
SERVANT OF THE SERVANTS OF GOD
TO ALL WHO READ THIS LETTER
MAY HOPE FILL YOUR HEARTS

1. *SPES NON CONFUNDIT.* "Hope does not disappoint" (*Rom* 5:5). In the spirit of hope, the Apostle Paul addressed these words of encouragement to the Christian community of Rome. Hope is also the central message of the coming Jubilee that, in accordance with an ancient tradition, the Pope proclaims every twenty-five years. My thoughts turn to all those *pilgrims of hope* who will travel to Rome in order to experience the Holy Year and to all those others who, though unable to visit the City of the Apostles Peter and Paul, will celebrate it in their local Churches. For everyone, may the Jubilee be a moment of genuine, personal encounter with the Lord Jesus, the "door" (cf. *Jn* 10:7.9) of our salvation, whom the Church is charged to

proclaim always, everywhere and to all as "our hope" (*1 Tim* 1:1).

Everyone knows what it is to hope. In the heart of each person, hope dwells as the desire and expectation of good things to come, despite our not knowing what the future may bring. Even so, uncertainty about the future may at times give rise to conflicting feelings, ranging from confident trust to apprehensiveness, from serenity to anxiety, from firm conviction to hesitation and doubt. Often we come across people who are discouraged, pessimistic and cynical about the future, as if nothing could possibly bring them happiness. For all of us, may the Jubilee be an opportunity to be renewed in hope. God's word helps us find reasons for that hope. Taking it as our guide, let us return to the message that the Apostle Paul wished to communicate to the Christians of Rome.

A word of hope
2. "Since we are justified through faith, we have peace with God through our Lord Jesus Christ, through whom we have obtained access to this grace in which we stand; and we boast in our hope of sharing in the glory of God... Hope does not disappoint, because God's love has been poured into our hearts through the Holy Spirit that has been given to us" (*Rom* 5:1-2.5). In this passage, Saint Paul gives us much to reflect upon. We know that the Letter to the Romans marked a decisive turning point in his work of evangelization. Until then, he had carried out his activity in the eastern part of the Empire, but now he turns to Rome and all that Rome meant in the eyes of the world. Before him lay a great challenge, which he took up for the sake of preaching the Gospel, which knows no barriers or confines. The Church of Rome was not founded by Paul, yet he felt impelled to hasten there in order to bring to everyone the Gospel of Jesus Christ, crucified and risen from the dead, a message of hope that fulfils

the ancient promises, leads to glory and, grounded in love, does not disappoint.

3. Hope is born of love and based on the love springing from the pierced heart of Jesus upon the cross: "For if while we were enemies, we were reconciled to God through the death of his Son, much more surely, having been reconciled, will we be saved by his life" (*Rom* 5:19). That life becomes manifest in our own life of faith, which begins with Baptism, develops in openness to God's grace and is enlivened by a hope constantly renewed and confirmed by the working of the Holy Spirit.

By his perennial presence in the life of the pilgrim Church, the Holy Spirit illumines all believers with the light of hope. He keeps that light burning, like an ever-burning lamp, to sustain and invigorate our lives. Christian hope does not deceive or disappoint because it is grounded in the certainty that nothing and no one may ever separate us from God's love: "Who will separate us from the love of Christ? Hardship, or distress, or persecution, or famine, or nakedness, or peril or the sword? No, in all these things we are more than conquerors through him who loved us. For I am convinced that neither death, nor life, nor angels, nor rulers, nor things present, nor things to come, nor powers, nor height, nor depth, nor anything else in all creation, will be able to separate us from the love of God in Christ Jesus our Lord" (*Rom* 8:35.37-39). Here we see the reason why this hope perseveres in the midst of trials: founded on faith and nurtured by charity, it enables us to press forward in life. As Saint Augustine observes: "Whatever our state of life, we cannot live without these three dispositions of the soul, namely, to believe, to hope and to love." [1]

4. Saint Paul is a realist. He knows that life has its joys and sorrows, that love is tested amid trials, and that hope can falter in the face of suffering. Even so, he can write: "We boast in our

27

sufferings, knowing that suffering produces endurance, and endurance produces character, and character produces hope" (*Rom* 5:3-4). For the Apostle, trials and tribulations mark the lives of those who preach the Gospel amid incomprehension and persecution (cf. *2 Cor* 6:3-10). Yet in those very contexts, beyond the darkness we glimpse a light: we come to realize that evangelization is sustained by the power flowing from Christ's cross and resurrection. In this way, we learn to practice a virtue closely linked to hope, namely *patience*. In our fast-paced world, we are used to wanting everything now. We no longer have time simply to be with others; even families find it hard to get together and enjoy one another's company. Patience has been put to flight by frenetic haste, and this has proved detrimental, since it leads to impatience, anxiety and even gratuitous violence, resulting in more unhappiness and self-centeredness.

Nor is there much place for patience in this age of the Internet, as space and time yield to an ever-present "now." Were we still able to contemplate creation with a sense of awe, we might better understand the importance of patience. We could appreciate the changes of the seasons and their harvests, observe the life of animals and their cycles of growth, and enjoy the clarity of vision of Saint Francis. In his *Canticle of the Creatures*, written exactly eight hundred years ago, Francis saw all creation as a great family and could call the sun his "brother" and the moon his "sister." [2] A renewed appreciation of the value of patience could only prove beneficial for ourselves and for others. Saint Paul often speaks of patience in the context of our need for perseverance and confident trust in God's promises. Yet, before all else, he testifies to God's own patience, as "the God of all patience and encouragement" (*Rom* 15:5). Patience, one of the fruits of the Holy Spirit, sustains our hope and strengthens it as a virtue and a way of life. May we learn to pray frequently for the grace of patience, which is both the daughter of hope and at the same time its firm foundation.

A journey of hope

5. This interplay of hope and patience makes us see clearly that the Christian life is a *journey* calling for *moments of greater intensity* to encourage and sustain hope as the constant companion that guides our steps towards the goal of our encounter with the Lord Jesus. I like to think that the proclamation of the first Jubilee, in the year 1300, was preceded by a journey of grace inspired by popular spirituality. How can we fail to recall the various ways by which the grace of forgiveness had been poured out upon God's holy and faithful People? We are reminded, for example, of the great "Pardon" that Saint Celestine V granted to all those who visited the Basilica of Santa Maria di Collemaggio in Aquila on the 28th and 29th days of August 1294, six years before Pope Boniface VIII instituted the Holy Year. The Church was already experiencing the grace of the Jubilee as an outpouring of divine mercy. Even earlier, in 1216, Pope Honorius III granted the plea of Saint Francis for an indulgence for all those visiting the Porziuncola on the first two days of August. The same can be said of the pilgrimage to Santiago de Compostela: in 1222, Pope Callistus II allowed the Jubilee to be celebrated there whenever the Feast of the Apostle James fell on a Sunday. It is good that such "dispersed" celebrations of the Jubilee continue, so that the power of God's forgiveness can support and accompany communities and individuals on their pilgrim way.

Pilgrimage is of course a fundamental element of every Jubilee event. Setting out on a journey is traditionally associated with our human quest for meaning in life. A pilgrimage on foot is a great aid for rediscovering the value of silence, effort and simplicity of life. In the coming year, *pilgrims of hope* will surely travel the ancient and more modern routes in order to experience the Jubilee to the full. In Rome itself, along with the usual visits to the catacombs and the Seven Churches, other itineraries of faith will be proposed. Journeying from one country to another as if borders no longer mattered, and passing from one city to another in contemplating the beauty of creation and masterpieces of art, we learn to treasure the richness of different experiences and cultures, and are inspired to lift up that beauty, in prayer, to God, in thanksgiving for his wondrous works. The Jubilee Churches along the pilgrimage routes and in the city of Rome can serve as oases of spirituality and places of rest on the pilgrimage of faith, where we can drink from the wellsprings of hope, above all by approaching the sacrament of Reconciliation, the essential starting-point of any true journey of conversion. In the particular Churches, special care should be taken to prepare priests and the faithful to celebrate the sacrament of Confession and to make it readily available in its individual form.

In a particular way, I would like to invite the faithful of the Eastern Churches, particularly those already in full communion with the Successor of Peter, to take part in this pilgrimage. They have suffered greatly, often even unto death, for their fidelity to Christ and the Church, and so they should feel themselves especially welcome in this City of Rome that is also their Mother and cherishes so many memories of their presence. The Catholic Church, enriched by their ancient liturgies and the theology and spirituality of their Fathers, monks and theologians, wants to give symbolic expression to its embrace of them and their Orthodox brothers and sisters in these times when they endure their own Way of the Cross, often forced by violence and instability to leave their homelands, their holy lands, for safer places. For them, the hope born of the knowledge that they are loved by the Church, which does not abandon them but follows them wherever they go, will make the symbolism of the Jubilee all the more powerful.

6. The Holy Year of 2025 is itself in continuity with preceding celebrations of grace. In the last Ordinary Jubilee, we crossed the threshold of two millennia from the birth of Jesus Christ. Then, on 13 March 2015, I proclaimed an Extraordinary Jubilee for the sake of making known and encouraging an encounter with the "merciful face of God," [3] the core message of the Gospel for every man and woman of every time and place. Now the time has come for a new Jubilee, when once more the Holy Door will be flung open to invite everyone to an intense experience of the love of God that awakens in hearts the sure hope of salvation in Christ. The Holy Year will also guide our steps towards yet another fundamental celebration for all Christians: 2033 will mark the two thousandth anniversary of the redemption won by the passion, death and resurrection of the Lord Jesus. We are about to make a pilgrimage marked by great events, in which the grace of God precedes and accompanies his people as they press forward firm in faith, active in charity and steadfast in hope (cf. *1 Thess* 1:3) .

Sustained by this great tradition, and certain that the Jubilee Year will be for the entire Church a lively experience of grace and hope, I hereby decree that the Holy Door of the Basilica of Saint Peter in the Vatican will be opened on 24 December 2024, thus inaugurating the Ordinary Jubilee. On the following Sunday, 29 December 2024, I will open the Holy Door of my cathedral, Saint John Lateran, which on 9 November this year will celebrate the 1700th anniversary of its dedication. Then, on 1 January 2025, the Solemnity of Mary, Mother of God, the Holy Door of the Papal Basilica of Saint Mary Major will be opened. Finally, Sunday, 5 January 2025, will mark the opening of the Holy Door of the Papal Basilica of Saint Paul outside the Walls. These last three Holy Doors will be closed on Sunday, 28 December 2025.

I further decree that on Sunday, 29 December 2024, in every cathedral and co-cathedral, diocesan bishops are to celebrate Holy Mass as the solemn opening of the Jubilee Year, using the ritual indications that will be provided for that occasion. For celebrations in co-cathedrals, the bishop's place can be taken by a suitably designated delegate. A pilgrimage that sets out from a church chosen for the *collectio* and then proceeds to the cathedral can serve to symbolize the journey of hope that, illumined by the word of God, unites all the faithful. In the course of this pilgrimage, passages from the present Document can be read, along with the announcement of the Jubilee Indulgence to be gained in accordance with the prescriptions found in the ritual indications mentioned above. The Holy Year will conclude in the particular Churches on Sunday, 28 December 2025; in the course of the year, every effort should be made to enable the People of God to participate fully in its proclamation of hope in God's grace and in the signs that attest to its efficacy.

The Ordinary Jubilee will conclude with the closing of the Holy Door in the Papal Basilica of Saint Peter in the Vatican on 6 January 2026, the Solemnity of the Epiphany of the Lord. During the Holy Year, may the light of Christian hope illumine every man and woman, as a message of God's love addressed to all! And may the Church bear faithful witness to this message in every part of the world!

Signs of hope

7. In addition to finding hope in God's grace, we are also called to discover hope in the *signs of the times* that the Lord gives us. As the Second Vatican Council observed: "In every age, the Church has the responsibility of reading the signs of the times and interpreting them in the light of the Gospel. In this way, in language adapted to every generation, she can respond to people's persistent questions about the meaning of this present life and of the life to come, and how one is related to the

other." [4] We need to recognize the immense goodness present in our world, lest we be tempted to think ourselves overwhelmed by evil and violence. The signs of the times, which include the yearning of human hearts in need of God's saving presence, ought to become signs of hope.

8. The first sign of hope should be the desire for *peace* in our world, which once more finds itself immersed in the tragedy of *war*. Heedless of the horrors of the past, humanity is confronting yet another ordeal, as many peoples are prey to brutality and violence. What does the future hold for those peoples, who have already endured so much? How is it possible that their desperate plea for help is not motivating world leaders to resolve the numerous regional conflicts in view of their possible consequences at the global level? Is it too much to dream that arms can fall silent and cease to rain down destruction and death? May the Jubilee remind us that those who are peacemakers will be called "children of God" (*Mt* 5:9). The need for peace challenges us all, and demands that concrete steps be taken. May diplomacy be tireless in its commitment to seek, with courage and creativity, every opportunity to undertake negotiations aimed at a lasting peace.

9. Looking to the future with hope also entails having enthusiasm for life and a readiness to share it. Sadly, in many situations this is lacking. A first effect of this is the *loss of the desire to transmit life*. A number of countries are experiencing an alarming *decline in the birthrate* as a result of today's frenetic pace, fears about the future, the lack of job security and adequate social policies, and social models whose agenda is dictated by the quest for profit rather than concern for relationships. In certain quarters, the tendency "to blame population growth, instead of extreme and selective consumerism on the part of some, is one way of refusing to face the [real] issues." [5]

Openness to life and responsible parenthood is the design that the Creator has implanted in the hearts and bodies of men and women, a mission that the Lord has entrusted to spouses and to their love. It is urgent that responsible legislation on the part of states be accompanied by the firm support of communities of believers and the entire civil community in all its components. For *the desire of young people to give birth to new sons and daughters* as a sign of the fruitfulness of their love ensures a future for every society. This is a matter of hope: it is born of hope and it generates hope.

Consequently, the Christian community should be at the forefront in pointing out the need for a *social covenant to support and foster hope*, one that is inclusive and not ideological, working for a future filled with the laughter of babies and children, in order to fill the empty cradles in so many parts of our world. All of us, however, need to recover the joy of living, since men and women, created in the image and likeness of God (cf. *Gen* 1:26), cannot rest content with getting along one day at a time, settling for the here and now and seeking fulfilment in material realities alone. This leads to a narrow individualism and the loss of hope; it gives rise to a sadness that lodges in the heart and brings forth fruits of discontent and intolerance.

10. During the Holy Year, we are called to be tangible signs of hope for those of our brothers and sisters who experience hardships of any kind. I think of *prisoners* who, deprived of their freedom, daily feel the harshness of detention and its restrictions, lack of affection and, in more than a few cases, lack of respect for their persons. I propose that in this Jubilee Year governments undertake initiatives aimed at restoring hope; forms of amnesty or pardon meant to help individuals regain confidence in themselves and in society; and programs of reintegration in the community, including a concrete commitment to respect for law.

This is an ancient appeal, one drawn from the word of God, whose wisdom remains ever timely. It calls for acts of clemency and liberation that enable new beginnings: "You shall hallow the fiftieth year and you shall proclaim liberty throughout the land to all its inhabitants" (*Lev* 25:10). This institution of the Mosaic law was later taken up by the prophet Isaiah: "The Lord has sent me to bring good news to the oppressed, to bind up the brokenhearted, to proclaim liberty to the captives and release to the prisoners, to proclaim the year of the Lord's favor" (*Is* 61:1-2). Jesus made those words his own at the beginning of his ministry, presenting himself as the fulfilment of the "year of the Lord's favor" (cf. *Lk* 4:18-19). In every part of the world, believers, and their Pastors in particular, should be one in demanding dignified conditions for those in prison, respect for their human rights and above all the abolition of the death penalty, a provision at odds with Christian faith and one that eliminates all hope of forgiveness and rehabilitation. [6] In order to offer prisoners a concrete sign of closeness, I would myself like to open a Holy Door in a prison, as a sign inviting prisoners to look to the future with hope and a renewed sense of confidence.

11. Signs of hope should also be shown to the *sick*, at home or in hospital. Their sufferings can be allayed by the closeness and affection of those who visit them. Works of mercy are also works of hope that give rise to immense gratitude. Gratitude should likewise be shown to all those healthcare workers who, often in precarious conditions, carry out their mission with constant care and concern for the sick and for those who are most vulnerable.

Inclusive attention should also be given to all those in particularly difficult situations, who experience their own weaknesses and limitations, especially those affected by illnesses or disabilities that severely restrict their personal independence and freedom. Care given to them is a hymn to human dignity, a song of hope that calls for the choral participation of society as a whole.

12. Signs of hope are also needed by those who are the very embodiment of hope, namely, *the young*. Sadly, they often see their dreams and aspirations frustrated. We must not disappoint them, for the future depends on their enthusiasm. It is gratifying to see the energy they demonstrate, for example, by rolling up their sleeves and volunteering to help when disasters strike and people are in need. Yet it is sad to see young people who are without hope, who face an uncertain and unpromising future, who lack employment or job security, or realistic prospects after finishing school. Without the hope that their dreams can come true, they will inevitably grow discouraged and listless. Escaping into drugs, risk-taking and the pursuit of momentary pleasure does greater harm to them in particular, since it closes them to life's beauty and richness, and can lead to depression and even self-destructive actions. For this reason, the Jubilee should inspire the Church to make greater efforts to reach out to them. With renewed passion, let us demonstrate care and concern for adolescents, students and young couples, the rising generation. Let us draw close to the young, for they are the joy and hope of the Church and of the world!

13. Signs of hope should also be present for *migrants* who leave their homelands behind in search of a better life for themselves and for their families. Their expectations must not be frustrated by prejudice and rejection. A spirit of welcome, which embraces everyone with respect for his or her dignity, should be accompanied by a sense of responsibility, lest anyone be denied the right to a dignified existence. *Exiles, displaced persons and refugees*, whom international tensions force to emigrate in order to avoid war, violence and discrimination, ought to be

guaranteed security and access to employment and education, the means they need to find their place in a new social context.

May the Christian community always be prepared to defend the rights of those who are most vulnerable, opening wide its doors to welcome them, lest anyone ever be robbed of the hope of a better future. May the Lord's words in the great parable of the Last Judgement always find an echo in our hearts: "I was a stranger and you welcomed me" for "just as you did it to one of the least of these my brothers and sisters, you did it to me" (*Mt* 25:35.40).

14. The *elderly*, who frequently feel lonely and abandoned, also deserve signs of hope. Esteem for the treasure that they are, their life experiences, their accumulated wisdom and the contribution that they can still make, is incumbent on the Christian community and civil society, which are called to cooperate in strengthening the covenant between generations.

Here I would also mention *grandparents*, who represent the passing on of faith and wisdom to the younger generation. May they find support in the gratitude of their children and the love of their grandchildren, who discover in them their roots and a source of understanding and encouragement.

15. I ask with all my heart that hope be granted to the billions of the *poor*, who often lack the essentials of life. Before the constant tide of new forms of impoverishment, we can easily grow inured and resigned. Yet we must not close our eyes to the dramatic situations that we now encounter all around us, not only in certain parts of the world. Each day we meet people who are poor or impoverished; they may even be our next-door neighbors. Often they are homeless or lack sufficient food for the day. They suffer from exclusion and indifference on the part of many. It is scandalous that in a world possessed of immense

resources, destined largely to producing weapons, the poor continue to be "the majority of the planet's population, billions of people. These days they are mentioned in international political and economic discussions, but one often has the impression that their problems are brought up as an afterthought, a question which gets added almost out of duty or in a tangential way, if not treated merely as collateral damage. Indeed, when all is said and done, they frequently remain at the bottom of the pile." [7] Let us not forget: the poor are almost always the victims, not the ones to blame.

Appeals for hope
16. Echoing the age-old message of the prophets, the Jubilee reminds us that *the goods of the earth* are not destined for a privileged few, but for everyone. The rich must be generous and not avert their eyes from the faces of their brothers and sisters in need. Here I think especially of those who lack water and food: hunger is a scandal, an open wound on the body of our humanity, and it summons all of us to a serious examination of conscience. I renew my appeal that "with the money spent on weapons and other military expenditures, let us establish a global fund that can finally put an end to hunger and favor development in the most impoverished countries, so that their citizens will not resort to violent or illusory situations, or have to leave their countries in order to seek a more dignified life." [8]

Another heartfelt appeal that I would make in light of the coming Jubilee is directed to the more affluent nations. I ask that they acknowledge the gravity of so many of their past decisions and determine to *forgive the debts* of countries that will never be able to repay them. More than a question of generosity, this is a matter of justice. It is made all the more serious today by a new form of injustice which we increasingly recognize, namely, that "a true 'ecological debt' exists, particularly between the global North and South, connected to commercial imbalances with effects on the environment and the disproportionate use of natural resources by certain countries over long periods of time." [9] As sacred Scripture teaches, the earth is the Lord's and all of us dwell in it as "aliens and tenants" (*Lev* 25:23). If we really wish to prepare a path to peace in our world, let us commit ourselves to remedying the remote causes of injustice, settling unjust and unpayable debts, and feeding the hungry.

17. The coming Jubilee Year will also coincide with a significant date for all Christians, namely, *the 1700ᵗʰ anniversary of the celebration of the first great Ecumenical Council, that of Nicaea*. It is worth noting that, from apostolic times, bishops have gathered on various occasions in order to discuss doctrinal questions and disciplinary matters. In the first centuries of Christianity, synods frequently took place in both East and West, showing the importance of ensuring the unity of God's People and the faithful proclamation of the Gospel. The Jubilee can serve as an important occasion for giving concrete expression to this form of synodality, which the Christian community today considers increasingly necessary for responding to the urgent need for evangelization. All the baptized, with their respective charisms and ministries, are co-responsible for ensuring that manifold signs of hope bear witness to God's presence in the world.

The Council of Nicaea sought to preserve the Church's unity, which was seriously threatened by the denial of the full divinity of Jesus Christ and hence his consubstantiality with the Father. Some three hundred bishops took part, convoked at the behest of the Emperor Constantine; their first meeting took place in the Imperial Palace on 20 May 325. After various debates, by the grace of the Spirit they unanimously approved the Creed that we still recite each Sunday at the celebration of the Eucharist. The Council Fathers chose to begin that Creed by using for the first time the expression " *We* believe," [10] as a sign that all the

Churches were in communion and that all Christians professed the same faith.

The Council of Nicaea was a milestone in the Church's history. The celebration of its anniversary invites Christians to join in a hymn of praise and thanksgiving to the Blessed Trinity and in particular to Jesus Christ, the Son of God, "consubstantial with the Father," [11] who revealed to us that mystery of love. At the same time, Nicaea represents a summons to all Churches and Ecclesial Communities to persevere on the path to visible unity and in the quest of fitting ways to respond fully to the prayer of Jesus "that they may all be one. As you, Father, are in me and I am in you, may they also be in us, so that the world may believe that you have sent me" (*Jn* 17:21).

The Council of Nicaea also discussed the date of Easter. To this day, different approaches to this question prevent celebrating the fundamental event of our faith on the same day. Providentially, a common celebration will take place in the year 2025. May this serve as an appeal to all Christians, East and West, to take a decisive step forward towards unity around a common date for Easter. We do well to remind ourselves that many people, unaware of the controversies of the past, fail to understand how divisions in this regard can continue to exist.

Anchored in hope
18. Hope, together with faith and charity, makes up the triptych of the "theological virtues" that express the heart of the Christian life (cf. *1 Cor* 13:13; *1 Thess* 1:3). In their inseparable unity, hope is the virtue that, so to speak, gives inward direction and purpose to the life of believers. For this reason, the Apostle Paul encourages us to "rejoice in hope, be patient in suffering, and persevere in prayer" (*Rom* 12:12). Surely we need to "abound in hope" (cf. *Rom* 15:13), so that we may bear credible and attractive witness to the faith and love that dwell in our

hearts; that our faith may be joyful and our charity enthusiastic; and that each of us may be able to offer a smile, a small gesture of friendship, a kind look, a ready ear, a good deed, in the knowledge that, in the Spirit of Jesus, these can become, for those who receive them, rich seeds of hope. Yet what is the basis of our hope? To understand this, let us stop and reflect on "the reasons for our hope" (cf. *1 Pet* 3:15).

19. "I believe in *life everlasting*." [12] So our faith professes. Christian hope finds in these words an essential foundation. For hope is "that theological virtue by which we desire... eternal life as our happiness." [13] The Second Vatican Council says of hope that, "when people are deprived of this divine support, and lack hope in eternal life, their dignity is deeply impaired, as may so often be seen today. The problems of life and death, of guilt and suffering, remain unsolved, so that people are frequently thrown into despair." [14] We, however, by virtue of the hope in which we were saved, can view the passage of time with the certainty that the history of humanity and our own individual history are not doomed to a dead end or a dark abyss, but directed to an encounter with the Lord of glory. As a result, we live our lives in expectation of his return and in the hope of living forever in him. In this spirit, we make our own the heartfelt prayer of the first Christians with which sacred Scripture ends: "Come, Lord Jesus!" (*Rev* 22:20).

20. The death and resurrection of Jesus is the heart of our faith and the basis of our hope. Saint Paul states this succinctly by the use of four verbs: "I handed on to you as of first importance what I in turn had received, that Christ died for our sins in accordance with the Scriptures, and that he was buried, and that he was raised on the third day in accordance with the Scriptures, and that he appeared to Cephas and then to the twelve" (*1 Cor* 15:3-5). Christ *died, was buried, was raised* and *appeared*. For our sake, Jesus experienced the drama of death. The Father's love

41

raised him in the power of the Spirit, and made of his humanity the first fruits of our eternal salvation. Christian hope consists precisely in this: that in facing death, which appears to be the end of everything, we have the certainty that, thanks to the grace of Christ imparted to us in Baptism, "life is changed, not ended," [15] forever. Buried with Christ in Baptism, we receive in his resurrection the gift of a new life that breaks down the walls of death, making it a passage to eternity.

The reality of *death*, as a painful separation from those dearest to us, cannot be mitigated by empty rhetoric. The Jubilee, however, offers us the opportunity to appreciate anew, and with immense gratitude, the gift of the new life that we have received in Baptism, a life capable of transfiguring death's drama. It is worth reflecting, in the context of the Jubilee, on how that mystery has been understood from the earliest centuries of the Church's life. An example would be the tradition of building baptismal fonts in the shape of an octagon, as seen in many ancient baptisteries, like that of Saint John Lateran in Rome. This was intended to symbolize that Baptism is the dawn of the "eighth day," the day of the resurrection, a day that transcends the normal, weekly passage of time, opening it to the dimension of eternity and to life everlasting: the goal to which we tend on our earthly pilgrimage (cf. *Rom* 6:22).

The most convincing testimony to this hope is provided by the *martyrs*. Steadfast in their faith in the risen Christ, they renounced life itself here below, rather than betray their Lord. Martyrs, as confessors of the life that knows no end, are present and numerous in every age, and perhaps even more so in our own day. We need to treasure their testimony, in order to confirm our hope and allow it to bear good fruit.

The martyrs, coming as they do from different Christian traditions, are also seeds of unity, expressions of the ecumenism of blood. I greatly hope that the Jubilee will also include ecumenical celebrations as a way of highlighting the richness of the testimony of these martyrs.

21. What, then, will become of us after death? With Jesus, beyond this threshold we will find eternal life, consisting in full communion with God as we forever contemplate and share in his infinite love. All that we now experience in hope, we shall then see in reality. We are reminded of the words of Saint Augustine: "When I am one with you in all my being, there will be no more pain and toil; my life shall be true life, a life wholly filled by you." [16] What will characterize this fullness of communion? Being happy. *Happiness* is our human vocation, a goal to which all aspire.

But what is happiness? What is the happiness that we await and desire? Not some fleeting pleasure, a momentary satisfaction that, once experienced, keeps us longing for more, in a desperate quest that leaves our hearts unsated and increasingly empty. We aspire to a happiness that is definitively found in the one thing that can bring us fulfilment, which is love. Thus, we will be able to say even now: I am loved, therefore I exist; and I will live forever in the love that does not disappoint, the love from which nothing can ever separate me. Let us listen once more to the words of the Apostle: "I am convinced that neither death, nor life, nor angels, nor rulers, nor things present, nor things to come, nor powers, nor height, nor depth, nor anything else in all creation, will be able to separate us from the love of God in Christ Jesus our Lord" (*Rom* 8:38-39).

22. Another reality having to do with eternal life is *God's judgement*, both at the end of our individual lives and at the end of history. Artists have often attempted to portray it – here we can think of Michelangelo's *magnum opus* in the Sistine Chapel – in accordance with the theological vision of their times and with

the aim of inspiring a sense of awe in the viewer. We should indeed prepare ourselves consciously and soberly for the moment when our lives will be judged, but we must always do this from the standpoint of hope, the theological virtue that sustains our lives and shields them from groundless fear. The judgement of God, who is love (cf. *1 Jn* 4:8.16), will surely be based on love, and in particular on all that we have done or failed to do with regard to those in need, in whose midst Christ, the Judge himself, is present (cf. *Mt* 25:31-46). Clearly, then, we are speaking of a judgement unlike any handed down by human, earthly tribunals; it should be understood as a rapport of truth with the God who is love and with oneself, within the unfathomable mystery of divine mercy. Sacred Scripture states: "You have taught your people that the righteous must be kind, and you have filled your children with good hope, because you give repentance for sins, so that… when we are judged, we may expect mercy" (*Wis* 12:19.22). In the words of Benedict XVI: "At the moment of judgement we experience and we absorb the overwhelming power of his love over all the evil in the world and in ourselves. The pain of love becomes our salvation and our joy." [17]

Judgement, then, concerns the salvation in which we hope and which Jesus has won for us by his death and resurrection. It is meant to bring us to a definitive encounter with the Lord. The evil we have done cannot remain hidden; it needs to be *purified* in order to enable this definitive encounter with God's love. Here we begin to see the need of our prayers for all those who have ended their earthly pilgrimage, our solidarity in an intercession that is effective by virtue of the communion of the saints, and the shared bond that makes us one in Christ, the firstborn of all creation. The Jubilee indulgence, thanks to the power of prayer, is intended in a particular way for those who have gone before us, so that they may obtain full mercy.

23. Indeed, the *indulgence* is a way of discovering the unlimited nature of God's mercy. Not by chance, for the ancients, the terms "mercy" and "indulgence" were interchangeable, as expressions of the fullness of God's forgiveness, which knows no bounds.

The *sacrament of Penance* assures us that God wipes away our sins. We experience those powerful and comforting words of the Psalm: "It is he who forgives all your guilt, who heals every one of your ills, who redeems your life from the grave, who crowns you with love and compassion... The Lord is compassion and love, slow to anger and rich in mercy... He does not treat us according to our sins, nor repay us according to our faults. For as the heavens are high above the earth, so strong is his love for those who fear him. As far as the east is from the west, so far does he remove our sins" (*Ps* 103:3-4.8.10-12). The sacrament of Reconciliation is not only a magnificent spiritual gift, but also a decisive, essential and fundamental step on our journey of faith. There, we allow the Lord to erase our sins, to heal our hearts, to raise us up, to embrace us and to reveal to us his tender and compassionate countenance. There is no better way to know God than to let him reconcile us to himself (cf. *2 Cor* 5:20) and savor his forgiveness. Let us not neglect Confession, but rediscover the beauty of this sacrament of healing and joy, the beauty of God's forgiveness of our sins!

Still, as we know from personal experience, every sin "leaves its mark." Sin has consequences, not only outwardly in the effects of the wrong we do, but also inwardly, inasmuch as "every sin, even venial, entails an unhealthy attachment to creatures, which must be purified either here on earth, or after death, in the state called Purgatory." [18] In our humanity, weak and attracted by evil, certain residual effects of sin remain. These are removed by the indulgence, always by the grace of Christ, who, as Saint Paul VI wrote, "is himself our 'indulgence'." [19] The Apostolic

Penitentiary will issue norms for obtaining and rendering spiritually fruitful the practice of the Jubilee indulgence.

This experience of full forgiveness cannot fail to open our hearts and minds to the need to *forgive others* in turn. Forgiveness does not change the past; it cannot change what happened in the past, yet it can allow us to change the future and to live different lives, free of anger, animosity and vindictiveness. Forgiveness makes possible a brighter future, which enables us to look at the past with different eyes, now more serene, albeit still bearing the trace of past tears.

For the last Extraordinary Jubilee, I commissioned *Missionaries of Mercy*, and these continue to carry out an important mission. During the coming Jubilee, may they exercise their ministry by reviving hope and offering forgiveness whenever a sinner comes to them with an open heart and a penitent spirit. May they remain a source of reconciliation and an encouragement to look to the future with heartfelt hope inspired by the Father's mercy. I encourage bishops to take advantage of their precious ministry, especially by sending them wherever hope is sorely tested: to prisons, hospitals, and places where people's dignity is violated, poverty abounds and social decay is prevalent. In this Jubilee Year, may no one be deprived of the opportunity to receive God's forgiveness and consolation.

24. Hope finds its supreme witness in *the Mother of God*. In the Blessed Virgin, we see that hope is not naive optimism but a gift of grace amid the realities of life. Like every mother, whenever Mary looked at her Son, she thought of his future. Surely she kept pondering in her heart the words spoken to her in the Temple by the elderly Simeon: "This child is destined for the falling and rising of many in Israel, and to be a sign that will be opposed, so that the inner thoughts of many will be revealed – and a sword will pierce your own soul too" (*Lk* 2:34-35). At the

foot of the cross, she witnessed the passion and death of Jesus, her innocent son. Overwhelmed with grief, she nonetheless renewed her "fiat," never abandoning her hope and trust in God. In this way, Mary cooperated for our sake in the fulfilment of all that her Son had foretold in announcing that he would have to "undergo great suffering, and be rejected by the elders, the chief priests, and the scribes, and be killed, and after three days rise again" (*Mk* 8:31). In the travail of that sorrow, offered in love, Mary became our Mother, the Mother of Hope. It is not by chance that popular piety continues to invoke the Blessed Virgin as *Stella Maris*, a title that bespeaks the sure hope that, amid the tempests of this life, the Mother of God comes to our aid, sustains us and encourages us to persevere in hope and trust.

In this regard, I would note that the Shrine of Our Lady of Guadalupe in Mexico City is preparing to celebrate, in 2031, the fifth centenary of Our Lady's first apparition. Through Juan Diego, the Mother of God brought a revolutionary message of hope that she continues to bring to every pilgrim and all the faithful: "Am I not here, who am your Mother?" [20] That message continues to touch hearts in the many Marian shrines throughout the world, where countless pilgrims commend to the holy Mother of God their cares, their sorrows and their hopes. During the Jubilee Year, may these shrines be sacred places of welcome and privileged spaces for the rebirth of hope. I encourage all pilgrims to Rome to spend time in prayer in the Marian shrines of the City, in order to venerate the Blessed Mother and to implore her protection. I am confident that everyone, especially the suffering and those most in need, will come to know the closeness of Mary, the most affectionate of mothers, who never abandons her children and who, for the holy people of God, is "a sign of certain hope and comfort." [21]

25. In our journey towards the Jubilee, let us return to Scripture and realize that it speaks to us in these words: "May we who have taken refuge in him be strongly encouraged to seize the hope set before us. We have this hope, a sure and steadfast anchor of the soul, a hope that enters the inner shrine behind the curtain, where Jesus, a forerunner on our behalf, has entered" (*Heb* 6:18-20). Those words are a forceful encouragement for us never to lose the hope we have been given, to hold fast to that hope and to find in God our refuge and our strength.

The image of the anchor is eloquent; it helps us to recognize the stability and security that is ours amid the troubled waters of this life, provided we entrust ourselves to the Lord Jesus. The storms that buffet us will never prevail, for we are firmly anchored in the hope born of grace, which enables us to live in Christ and to overcome sin, fear and death. This hope, which transcends life's fleeting pleasures and the achievement of our immediate goals, makes us rise above our trials and difficulties, and inspires us to keep pressing forward, never losing sight of the grandeur of the heavenly goal to which we have been called.

The coming Jubilee will thus be a Holy Year marked by the hope that does not fade, our hope in God. May it help us to recover the confident trust that we require, in the Church and in society, in our interpersonal relationships, in international relations, and in our task of promoting the dignity of all persons and respect for God's gift of creation. May the witness of believers be for our world a leaven of authentic hope, a harbinger of new heavens and a new earth (cf. *2 Pet* 3:13), where men and women will dwell in justice and harmony, in joyful expectation of the fulfilment of the Lord's promises.

Let us even now be drawn to this hope! Through our witness, may hope spread to all those who anxiously seek it. May the way we live our lives say to them in so many words: "Hope in the Lord! Hold firm, take heart and hope in the Lord!" (*Ps* 27:14). May the power of hope fill our days, as we await with confidence the coming of the Lord Jesus Christ, to whom be praise and glory, now and forever.

---

[1] *Serm.* 198 augm. 2.

[2] Cf. *Fonti Francescane*, No. 263, 6.10.

[3] Cf. Bull of Indiction of the Extraordinary Jubilee of Mercy *Misericordiae Vultus*, 1-3.

[4] Pastoral Constitution *Gaudium et Spes*, 4.

[5] Encyclical Letter *Laudato Si'*, 50.

[6] Cf. *Catechism of the Catholic Church*, No. 2267.

[7] Encyclical Letter *Laudato Si'*, 49

[8] Encyclical Letter *Fratelli Tutti*, 262.

[9] Encyclical Letter *Laudato Si'*, 51.

[10] Nicene Creed: H. DENZINGER-A. SCHÖNMETZER, *Enchiridion symbolorum definitionum et declarationum de rebus fidei et morum*, 125.

[11] Ibid.

[12] Apostles' Creed: H. DENZINGER-A. SCHÖNMETZER, *Enchiridion symbolorum definitionum et declarationum de rebus fidei et morum*, 30.

[13] *Catechism of the Catholic Church*, No. 1817.

[14] Pastoral Constitution *Gaudium et Spes*, 21.

[15] ROMAN MISSAL , *Preface I for the Dead.*

[16] *Confessions*, X, 28.

[17] Encyclical Letter *Spe Salvi*, 47.

[18] *Catechism of the Catholic Church*, No. 1472.

[19] Apostolic Letter *Apostolorum Limina*, 23 May 1974, II.

[20] *Nican Mopohua*, No. 119.

[21] SECOND VATICAN ECUMENICAL COUNCIL, Dogmatic Constitution *Lumen Gentium*, 68.

https://www.vatican.va/content/francesco/en/bulls/docume
nts/20240509_spes-non-confundit_bolla-giubileo2025.html

(Dicastero per la Comunicazione - Libreria Editrice Vaticana)

Letter of Pope Francis

TO MSGR. RINO FISICHELLA, PRESIDENT OF THE
PONTIFICAL COUNCIL FOR THE PROMOTION OF
THE NEW EVANGELIZATION, FOR THE JUBILEE
2025

To My Dear Brother the Most Reverend Rino Fisichella
president of the Pontifical Council for the Promotion of the
New Evangelization:

The Jubilee has always been an event of great spiritual, ecclesial,
and social significance in the life of the Church. Ever since 1300,
when Boniface VIII instituted the first Holy Year – initially
celebrated every hundred years, then, following its biblical
precedent, every fifty years, and finally every twenty-five years –
God's holy and faithful people has experienced this celebration
as a special gift of grace, characterized by the forgiveness of sins
and in particular by the indulgence, which is a full expression of
the mercy of God. The faithful, frequently at the conclusion of
a lengthy pilgrimage, draw from the spiritual treasury of the
Church by passing through the Holy Door and venerating the
relics of the Apostles Peter and Paul preserved in Roman
basilicas. Down the centuries, millions upon millions of pilgrims
have journeyed to these sacred places, bearing living witness to
the faith professed in every age.

The Great Jubilee of the year 2000 ushered the Church into the
third millennium of her history. Saint John Paul II had long
awaited and greatly looked forward to that event, in the hope
that all Christians, putting behind their historical divisions, could
celebrate together the two thousandth anniversary of the birth
of Jesus Christ, the Savior of humanity. Now, as the first twenty-
five years of the new century draw to a close, we are called to
enter into a season of preparation that can enable the Christian

people to experience the Holy Year in all its pastoral richness. A significant step on this journey was already taken with the celebration of the Extraordinary Jubilee of Mercy, which allowed us to appreciate anew all the power and tenderness of the Father's merciful love, in order to become, in our turn, its witnesses.

In the last two years, not a single country has been unaffected by the sudden outbreak of an epidemic that made us experience first-hand not only the tragedy of dying alone, but also the uncertainty and fleetingness of existence, and in doing so, has changed our very way of life. Together with all our brothers and sisters, we Christians endured those hardships and limitations. Our churches remained closed, as did our schools, factories, offices, shops, and venues for recreation. All of us saw certain freedoms curtailed, while the pandemic generated feelings not only of grief, but also, at times, of doubt, fear and disorientation. The scientific community quickly developed an initial remedy that is gradually permitting us to resume our daily lives. We are fully confident that the epidemic will be overcome and that the world will return to its usual pattern of personal relationships and social life. This will happen more readily to the extent that we can demonstrate effective solidarity, so that our neighbors most in need will not be neglected, and that everyone can have access to scientific breakthroughs and the necessary medicines.

We must fan the flame of hope that has been given us, and help everyone to gain new strength and certainty by looking to the future with an open spirit, a trusting heart and far-sighted vision. The forthcoming Jubilee can contribute greatly to restoring a climate of hope and trust as a prelude to the renewal and rebirth that we so urgently desire; that is why I have chosen as the motto of the Jubilee, Pilgrims of Hope. This will indeed be the case if we are capable of recovering a sense of universal fraternity and refuse to turn a blind eye to the tragedy of rampant poverty that prevents millions of men, women, young people and children from living in a manner worthy of our human dignity. Here I think in particular of the many refugees forced to abandon their native lands. May the voices of the poor be heard throughout this time of preparation for the Jubilee, which is meant to restore access to the fruits of the earth to everyone. As the Bible teaches, "The sabbath of the land shall provide food for you, for yourself and for your male and female slaves and for your hired servant and the sojourner who lives with you; for your cattle also, and for the beasts that are in your land, all its yield shall be for food" (Lev 25:6-7).

The spiritual dimension of the Jubilee, which calls for conversion, should also embrace these fundamental aspects of our life in society as part of a coherent whole. In the realization that all of us are pilgrims on this earth, which the Lord has charged us to till and keep (cf. Gen 2:15), may we never fail, in the course of our sojourn, to contemplate the beauty of creation and care for our common home. It is my hope that the coming Jubilee Year will be celebrated and experienced with this intention too. Growing numbers of men and women, including many young people and children, have come to realize that care for creation is an essential expression of our faith in God and our obedience to his will.

To you, dear Brother, I entrust responsibility for finding suitable ways for the Holy Year to be planned and celebrated with deep faith, lively hope and active charity. The Dicastery charged with promoting the new evangelization can help make this season of grace a significant stimulus to the pastoral outreach of the particular Churches, both Latin and Eastern, which are called in these years to intensify their commitment to synodality. In this regard, our pilgrimage towards the Jubilee will express and confirm the shared journey that the Church is called to make, in order to be ever more fully a sign and instrument of unity in harmonious diversity. It will be important to foster a renewed awareness of the demands of the universal call to responsible participation by enhancing the charisms and ministries that the Holy Spirit never ceases to bestow for the building up of the one Church. The four Constitutions of the Second Vatican Ecumenical Council, together with the Magisterium of these recent decades, will continue to provide direction and guidance to God's holy people, so that it can press forward in its mission of bringing the joyful proclamation of the Gospel to everyone.

As is customary, the Bull of Indiction, to be issued in due course, will contain the necessary guidelines for celebrating the Jubilee of 2025. In this time of preparation, I would greatly desire that we devote 2024, the year preceding the Jubilee event, to a great "symphony" of prayer. Prayer, above all else, to renew our desire to be in the presence of the Lord, to listen to him and to adore him. Prayer, moreover, to thank God for the many gifts of his love for us and to praise his work in creation, which summons everyone to respect it and to take concrete and responsible steps to protect it. Prayer as the expression of a single "heart and soul" (cf. Acts 4:32), which then translates into solidarity and the sharing of our daily bread. Prayer that makes it possible for every man and woman in this world to turn to the one God and to reveal to him what lies hidden in the depths of their heart. Prayer as the royal road to holiness, which enables us to be contemplative even in the midst of activity. In a word, may it be an intense year of prayer in which hearts are opened to receive the outpouring of God's grace and to make the "Our Father," the prayer Jesus taught us, the life program of each of his disciples.

I ask the Blessed Virgin Mary to accompany the Church on the journey of preparation for the grace-filled event of the Jubilee, and to you and your co-workers, with gratitude, I cordially send my Blessing.

Rome, Saint John Lateran, 11 February 2022, Memorial of the Blessed Virgin Mary of Lourdes.

FRANCIS

https://www.iubilaeum2025.va/en/giubileo-2025/lettera-di-papa-francesco.html

(Dicastero per la Comunicazione - Libreria Editrice Vaticana)

The Jubilee Prayer
Pope Francis

Father in heaven,
may the faith you have given us
in your son, Jesus Christ, our brother,
and the flame of charity enkindled
in our hearts by the Holy Spirit,
reawaken in us the blessed hope
for the coming of your Kingdom.

May your grace transform us
into tireless cultivators of the seeds of the Gospel.
May those seeds transform from within both humanity and the
whole cosmos
in the sure expectation
of a new heaven and a new earth,
when, with the powers of Evil vanquished,
your glory will shine eternally.

May the grace of the Jubilee
reawaken in us, Pilgrims of Hope,
a yearning for the treasures of heaven.
May that same grace spread
the joy and peace of our Redeemer
throughout the earth.

To you our God, eternally blessed,
be glory and praise for ever.
Amen

https://www.jubilaeum2025.va/en/giubileo-
2025/preghiera.html

The Jubilee Logo

The logo depicts four colored, stylized figures. They represent all of humanity, coming from the four corners of the earth. They embrace each other to indicate the solidarity and fraternity that should unite all peoples. The figure at the front is embracing the cross. It is not only the sign of the faith that this lead figure embraces but also of hope, which can never be abandoned, because we are always in need of hope, especially in our moments of greatest need.

Beneath the figures are rough waves. This symbolizes the fact that the pilgrimage of life is not always smooth. Often, daily life and events in the wider world require a greater call to hope. Thus, the lower part of the cross has been elongated and converted into the shape of an anchor, which is let down into the waves. The anchor is well known as a symbol of hope. In maritime jargon, the "anchor of hope" refers to the reserve anchor used as an emergency maneuver to stabilize the ship during storms.

In sum, the logo illustrates that the pilgrim's journey is not an individual undertaking but is something communal. It is marked by an increasing dynamism that leads believers ever closer to the cross. The cross in the logo is not static; rather, it is dynamic. It bends down towards humanity, not leaving human beings alone but stretching out to them to offer the certainty of its presence and the security of hope.

At the bottom of the logo is the motto of the 2025 Jubilee Year: *Peregrinates in Spem* (Pilgrims in Hope), represented in green letters.

https://www.iubilaeum2025.va/en/giubileo-2025/logo.html

Hymn for the 2025 Jubilee

Pilgrims of Hope

[Click here to listen.]
[https://youtu.be/7uXO8lUcEZI]

(Original text: Pierangelo Sequeri
English translation: Andrew Wadsworth)

**Like a flame my hope is burning,
may my song arise to you:
Source of life that has no ending,
on life's path I trust in you.**

Ev'ry nation, tongue, and people
find a light within your Word.
Scattered fragile sons and daughters
find a home in your dear Son.

**Like a flame my hope is burning,
may my song arise to you:
Source of life that has no ending,
on life's path I trust in you.**

God, so tender and so patient,
dawn of hope, you care for all.
Heav'n and earth are recreated
by the Spirit of Life set free.

**Like a flame my hope is burning,
may my song arise to you:
Source of life that has no ending,
on life's path I trust in you.**

Raise your eyes, the wind is blowing,

for our God is born in time.
Son made man for you and many
who will find the way in him.

**Like a flame my hope is burning,
may my song arise to you:
Source of life that has no ending,
on life's path I trust in you.**

Part II: Visiting Rome

A Brief History of Rome

The city of Rome is unparalleled in the annals of world history. It was once a world empire; it has a long Christian history and is today the seat of the Catholic Church; it has an immense artistic heritage; and it is today a modern capital metropolis.

View of the Roman Forum from the Capitoline Museums in Rome by Wolfgang Moroder (CC BY-SA 3.0)

Aptly termed the Eternal City, according to tradition, Rome was founded in 753 B.C. when the mythic twin brothers Romulus and Remus—raised by a she-wolf—delineated the city's boundaries. After committing fratricide, Romulus lent his name to the new city, *Roma*. What began as a small kingdom of settlements on Rome's storied seven hills eventually morphed into a successful city-state governed by the S.P.Q.R. (Senate and Roman People). Centuries later, after a series of wars (some civil, many foreign), Octavian emerged as the sole ruler of Rome, taking the name Caesar Augustus.

At its height in the early second century A.D., the Roman Empire spanned three continents, including Asia Minor, North Africa, and much of Europe. It extended west as far as Spain and France, north as far as Britain and Germany to the Rhine, south as far as North Africa, and east to include Dalmatia, Greece, Syria, Palestine, Turkey, Armenia, and ancient Babylon.

The name Rome was synonymous with a mighty military, extraordinary feats of engineering, and massive buildings.

At the same time, a poor Hebrew child was born in a backwater Roman province known as Palestine. Jesus' preaching, teachings, and healings, followed by his Passion, death, and Resurrection were about to turn the Roman world upside down. The polytheistic religions were too deeply entrenched and enshrined with Roman citizenship to allow for belief in a jealous Hebrew deity that would not allow for the required annual sacrifice to the three Roman deities of Jupiter, Juno, and Minerva.

Religion in Italy and throughout the Mediterranean basin in that era was mostly pagan. Different gods had different functions, the ancients believed, involving everything from life to death, health to childbirth, and weather to the crops. The natural world, cities, homes, and families were believed to be animated by a particular god or gods. Worship and devotions followed local customs and traditions, and paganism lacked universal creeds or a sense of orthodoxy.

The Jews were the exception. Though they held to a monotheistic belief in one God, they were exempt from the Roman requirement to sacrifice to the Roman gods. The early Christian community continued to observe Jewish customs and laws, and the Good News that the longed-for Messiah had come was initially preached by Jews to fellow Jews in the synagogues. As Christianity was considered by Roman authorities to be a subsect of Judaism, Christians too were initially tolerated. When Sts. Peter and Paul came to Rome in the early 60s, things had changed. According to Scripture, St. Paul came to Rome to defend himself in court (see Acts 28:11-31). St. Peter's sojourn in Rome is not clear in Scripture, though an early tradition places him in Rome as leader of the Church.

When a fire destroyed a large part of Rome in 64 A.D., Emperor Nero used it as an excuse to blame the Christians. He famously played his fiddle while Rome burned. Christians were now considered subversive. Not only would they not participate in the annual sacrifice to the Roman gods, but their teachings were spreading among the Gentiles, or non-Jews. With that, a long era of persecution began.

Sts. Peter and Paul were martyred in Rome in the initial wave. On the *Mons Vaticanus*, or Vatican Hill, there was a minor stadium used for spectacles and public executions. According to tradition, St. Peter was crucified upside down in that stadium. After his death, the Christian community buried him in a nearby necropolis. Like Peter, Paul's preaching was also causing turmoil, and according to Scripture, he was brought to Rome to stand trial. Like St. Peter, it is believed that he was martyred in Rome. According to tradition, he was beheaded on the Via Ostiense, the road from Rome to the port city of Ostia.

Over the next two and a half centuries, the persecutions ebbed and flowed, alternating between unspeakable cruelty and quiet tolerance. The most ruthless emperors were Caligula, Diocletian, and Galerius. The persecutions ended with Emperor Constantine and the famous Edict of Milan, which decriminalized Christianity. He set the stage for broad acceptance of the formerly banned religion by constructing grandiose churches throughout Rome and beyond. He built basilicas over the sites where it was believed that Peter and Paul were buried. He built a basilica in honor of St. Mary the Great, as well as a cathedral in honor of St. John. Finally, in 380 A.D., under Emperor Theodosius and the Edict of Thessalonica, Christianity became the official state religion of Rome.

Throughout antiquity, the bishops of Rome enjoyed a preeminent position among the ancient Churches. They became known as popes (from the Greek word *páppas*, meaning "father"). The preeminence of the See of Rome was due in part to Rome's legacy as the capital of the ancient world. Moreover, it was the city where countless Roman martyrs sacrificed their lives, including Sts. Peter and Paul. Most important, as apostolic successors of St. Peter, the popes were direct apostolic successors to St. Peter, who was named leader of the early Church by Christ himself (see Matthew 16:18).

When the Roman Empire officially fell (476 A.D. is given as the date, as it was the year in which the last Roman emperor was deposed and a Germanic emperor was installed), Rome officially entered the Middle Ages. With more conversions of the Greco-Roman peoples to Christianity, the Church continued to grow in influence and authority, and the popes and Church began to assume more and more social roles. Despite the temporary absences of the popes who lived in other central Italian cities (and sometimes even France), Rome was known primarily as a papal city.

In the late classical/early medieval period, Rome suffered frequent barbarian invasions. In the late eighth century, the French kings offered their support. In 781, Charlemagne, the King of the Franks, established a buffer zone around the city over which he granted temporal rule to the pope. In return, in 800 A.D., Pope Leo III crowned Charlemagne as the Holy Roman Emperor. By governing Rome and surrounding territories under the protection of the French crown, the pope acquired a secondary role in addition to being the spiritual leader of the Catholic Church. The pope was now the temporal ruler of the Territories of the Church, also known as the Papal States. The symbol of the papacy was two keys, representing the power to bind and loose on earth (silver) and in Heaven (gold), in reference to Matthew 16:18-19.

The power and size of the Papal States waxed and waned over the centuries, depending on the political acumen of the pope as well as that of neighboring sovereigns and rulers. While central Italy was governed by the pope, the rest of the peninsula was a hodgepodge of city-states, kingdoms, and principalities, along with some areas controlled by foreign rulers.

During the Renaissance, popes, cardinals, and the nobility called on the best artists to embellish their churches, chapels, and palaces. After the sixteenth-century Council of Trent (instituted as a response to the Protestant Reformation), the Catholic Church entered the Counter-Reformation. During this period and the subsequent Baroque era, the Roman cityscape underwent dramatic transformations in architecture and art. Grandiose new churches were built by new religious orders charged with spreading the Gospel far and wide, while existing churches, including St. Peter's Basilica, were reimagined according to the updated mission of the Catholic Church.

The nineteenth century was a difficult period for the popes and the Catholic Church in general throughout Italy, especially the monasteries and convents. In the early part of the century, Napoleon invaded Italy and instituted the first suppression of the Catholic Church. After Napoleon's defeat at Waterloo, Italian nationalists and revolutionaries like Mazzini and Garibaldi, inspired by French republican ideals, began to call for a politically unified Italy, a movement called the Risorgimento.

Pope Pius IX fiercely opposed the Risorgimento, especially as the future Kingdom of Italy would include the annexation of the Papal States. He believed that nationalism, liberalism, and democracy were fruits of the Enlightenment and that man was not capable of ruling himself. Therefore, he resisted the Risorgimento with every tool at his disposal. The pope's defeat took place on September 20, 1871, when the Roman city gate of Porta Pia was breached in what is known as the Capture of Rome. With that, almost eleven centuries of papal control over Rome and the surrounding territories came to an end. Instead of ruling the Papal States, the pope was now a prisoner of the Vatican. As happened during the Napoleonic period, the newly united Kingdom of Italy instituted another suppression, and Catholic orders found their properties once again confiscated by the government.

This sad state of affairs between the Catholic Church and the Italian kingdom was finally reconciled in 1929 with the Lateran Accords. This treaty between Pope Pius XI and Mussolini led to the creation of an autonomous Vatican city-state, which granted the Holy See full and independent sovereignty. The Church was granted other privileges, including the collection of a Church income tax and control over certain societal mores, such as marriage and religious education in public schools.

In later decades, some of these privileges were revoked through referendums or legislation. Italy's new Constitution after World War II removed the Catholic Church's title as the designated state religion of Italy, and the country became known as a "lay republic." Two referenda in the early 1980s stripped more power from the Church while legalizing abortion and artificial contraception.

Given the city's three millennia of history, contemporary Rome is fascinating to the point of being dizzying. A visit to the city today reveals vestiges of a once glorious empire succeeded by Christianity, supplanted, in turn, by a modern, secularized cosmopolitan city. UNESCO captured this dichotomy well when it declared the historic center of Rome a World Heritage Site in 1980 for the "major monuments of antiquity such as the Forums, the Mausoleum of Augustus, the Mausoleum of Hadrian, the Pantheon, Trajan's Column, and the Column of Marcus Aurelius, as well as the religious and public buildings of papal Rome."

Today, with a population of some 4 million residents trying to live and work in a modern city superimposed on three millennia of history, Rome is characterized by traffic congestion, noise, and disorganization—though some would describe the Roman experience as "pure chaos." Indeed, pickpockets, petty thieves, and dishonest taxi drivers only add to the challenges a modern pilgrim faces in Rome. Yet, if visitors can look beyond Rome's graffiti-covered walls, overflowing trash bins, and potholed streets, they will experience a place filled with spiritual and material treasures of every kind. Pilgrims can spend weeks, even months, in Rome and not take everything in.

In fact, for the Catholic pilgrim, there is no place in the world like Rome. With its unparalleled history, innumerable churches, countless saints and martyrs, and history of popes, it is a vital part of any pilgrimage experience in Italy. In Rome, pilgrims can visit Vatican City—a politically autonomous microstate that serves as the headquarters of the Catholic Church—to pay homage to Sts. Peter and Paul at their tombs, venerate the early martyrs in the catacombs, learn about Catholic history, discover beautiful churches, and learn about the saints and founders of religious orders scattered throughout the city.

Jubilee Itineraries

The Jubilee Churches

Numerous churches have been designated as gathering points for pilgrims. Various activities will take place in these churches, such as catechesis on the meaning of the Holy Year. Teachings will be conducted in different languages. These churches will also offer the sacrament of reconciliation and prayers.

Visit this link for more on the official Jubilee churches: www.iubilaeum2025.va/en/pellegrinaggio/le-chiese-giubilari.html

The Seven Churches Itinerary

One of the most memorable ways to explore the Christian history of Rome is by visiting what are known as the Seven Churches of Rome. The route dates to the sixteenth century, when St. Philip Neri began walking the route as a personal devotion. He soon began attracting crowds, particularly during Lent. At each church, the popular saint would lead prayer, sing, and offer a reflection, followed by food and beverages.

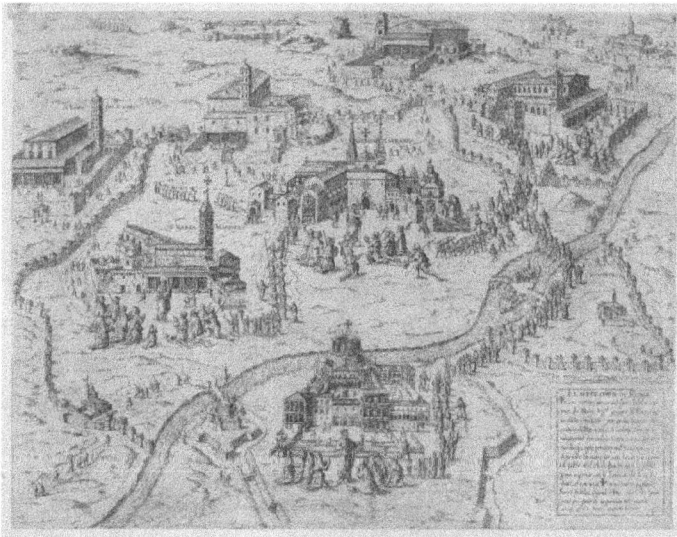

A 16th-century map of the Seven Churches of Rome, 1575 (Public Domain).

The itinerary consists of Rome's four Major Basilicas (also known as Papal or Patriarchal Basilicas): St. Peter's, St. Paul outside the Walls, St. John in Lateran, and St. Mary Major. It also includes the three Minor Basilicas: St. Sebastian's, Holy Cross in Jerusalem, and St. Lawrence outside the Walls. The itinerary remains popular with contemporary pilgrims, as the seven churches are the most significant Christian sites in Rome. The route—roughly twenty kilometers (13 mi)—is by and large the same as in centuries past. However, Rome's modern urban landscape has considerably altered the experience. St. Philip Neri and his companions did not have to share narrow Roman streets with crazed taxi drivers and speeding Vespas. Moreover, the obelisks in front of the churches, once the highest structures in the city and visible points of reference, are today obscured by tall, nineteenth-century apartment buildings. So while the entire walk can still be accomplished in a day, most modern pilgrims choose to do it in two or more days. Likewise, while fervent pilgrims choose to walk all of it, others take shortcuts by using taxis or public transportation for the rest.

St. Peter's (*San Pietro*)

The Seven Churches of Rome itinerary begins at the renowned Basilica of St. Peter in Vatican City. Built over the tomb and remains of St. Peter, the edifice is a testament to Christ's words to St. Peter in the Gospel: "You are Peter, and upon this rock I will build my church" (Matthew 16:18). This verse is written in large letters around the interior of the dome in Latin and Greek letters. The use of the two main languages from antiquity was done purposefully as an announcement to the entire world.

St. Peter's Square during a Papal Audience. (Courtesy of Bret Thoman)

Though not mentioned in Scripture, ancient texts and traditions refer to St. Peter's execution on Vatican Hill during the persecutions of Emperor Nero in 64 A.D. After the local Christian community buried St. Peter in a nearby necropolis, they erected an inconspicuous shrine (known as a trophaeum, in Greek) to mark the spot. When Emperor Constantine legalized Christianity, he ordered a large basilica built over the existing monument. During the fifteenth century, in the Renaissance era, the Constantinian basilica was razed and the current church was built. Archaeological excavations conducted in the early part of the twentieth century under Pope Pius XI confirmed Peter's tomb and his relics. (The necropolis and a part of St. Peter's tomb can be visited during the Scavi tour.)

There are a number of venerated relics within St. Peter's, although they are not visible to the public. In the four massive pillars surrounding the main altar and supporting the dome are niches designed by Baroque architect Bernini: the Veil of Veronica, part of the True Cross, a piece of the Holy Lance, and the skull of St. Andrew the Apostle. Reliefs sculpted within marble illustrate the specific relic contained inside. There are also three relics of the Passion in the chapel above the statue of

St. Veronica. During Holy Week, they are used to bless the faithful.

Highlights within St. Peter's Basilica include the Pietà (one of Michelangelo's most famous sculptures), the tombs of the popes (known as the Vatican Grottoes), and relics and statues of saints. The focal point in the nave is the main altar beneath Bernini's monumental bronze baldachin, or canopy. Beneath it is a recessed area known as the *confessio* (where St. Peter "confessed" his faith in Christ). St. Peter's tomb is deep beneath it.

Plan your visit:
Address: Piazza San Pietro, Vatican City
Website: www.basilicasanpietro.va/en.html

St. Paul's outside the Walls (*San Paolo fuori le Mura*)

The next stop is to the Basilica of St. Paul's outside the Walls to visit the tomb of Rome's other patron saint. (Sts. Peter and Paul are celebrated as one feast together on June 29.) Recent archaeological excavations conducted in the early 2000s have confirmed the tomb of St. Paul beneath the main altar of the basilica. Similar to the trajectory of St. Peter, when Paul was executed, his followers erected a nondescript memorial cell over the site of his tomb. In the fourth century, Constantine built a larger basilica over the burial shrine.

The courtyard of St. Paul's outside the Walls. (Courtesy of Bret Thoman)

The Basilica of Saint Paul is one of Rome's most majestic churches. Though the basilica dates to antiquity, the extant church was almost entirely rebuilt in 1826 after the previous one was destroyed in a fire. As it is outside the city center, it is generally less crowded than the downtown basilicas, and many visitors say it has a more spiritual ambience.

Upon arrival, visitors are greeted by impressive façade mosaics with golden reflections, colonnades, and a quadrilateral portico, enclosing a grassy area with a monumental statue of St. Paul in the center. The interior features a spacious nave and two side aisles, separated by eighty columns. Of note are the basilica's coffered ceiling, series of medallions with portraits of the popes, and apse and arch mosaics. Below the Gothic-era canopy, adjacent to the main altar, is the recessed *confessio* (also named after the "confession" of the apostle's faith). Here is the tomb of St. Paul. Also displayed is a chain believed to have held him in custody. Just beyond the exit off the right transept is an archaeological site for a fee.

Plan your visit:
Address: Piazzale San Paolo, 1 Rome
Website: www.basilicasanpaolo.org/en

The Cathedral of St. John in Lateran (_La Cattedrale di San Giovanni in Laterano_)

The Basilica of St. John in Lateran is perhaps the most significant Christian site in Rome. Not only is St. John in Lateran the cathedral church for the diocese of Rome, but it is also considered the Mother Church of all Christendom in that it has primacy over all other sees. Beginning with Pope Sylvester I in the early fourth century through the early fourteenth century, popes lived in a lavish palace adjacent to the extant cathedral. The tradition ended when the French pope Clement V moved the papal court to Avignon, France, in 1309. When the pope returned from France to Rome in the late fourteenth century, the Lateran Palace was too damaged to house the papacy, so the pope constructed and took up residence in the Apostolic Palace next to St. Peter's Basilica.

The Façade of St. John in Lateran. (Courtesy of Bret Thoman)

The Cathedral of St. John in Lateran is an edifice worthy to house the chair of the Bishop of Rome and deserving of its status as "mother and head of all the churches in the city and the world," as inscribed on a plaque on the front wall. On the left side of the portico is a large statue of Emperor Constantine, suggesting a connection between the ancient Roman emperor and the papacy. The interior is majestic. It includes Cosmatesque floors, brilliant mosaics in the apse and arch, monumental statues of the twelve apostles throughout the nave, a gilded wooden ceiling, and a majestic high altar and canopy over the *confessio*. The fourteenth-century Gothic ciborium (canopy) contains a relic of what is believed to have been the original wooden altar used by St. Peter. It also contains two images of Sts. Peter and Paul, the patron saints of Rome.

Not far from the cathedral is the octagonal Lateran baptistery, which was founded by Pope Sixtus III in the early sixth century. For many centuries, it was the only baptistery in Rome. It is decorated with precious materials and embellished with art from the Middle Ages through the Renaissance.

Just across the busy street from the Lateran Cathedral is another revered pilgrimage site. The Sanctuary of the Holy Stairs houses what is believed to be the twenty-eight-step staircase on which Jesus was judged by Pontius Pilate in Jerusalem. According to tradition, Helena, the mother of Constantine, had the stairs brought to Rome after her pilgrimage to the Holy Land in the early fourth century. Many pilgrims climb up the stairs on their knees in an act of devotion.

At the top of the staircase is a chapel known as the Sancta Sanctorum (Holy of Holies). Behind an iron grating is an icon considered to be the most venerated image in Rome since medieval times. It is known as the Acheropita, an image of the Holy Savior meaning "not painted by human hand." Recently, the papal chapel housing the icon has been opened to the public.
Plan your visit:
Address: Piazza S. Giovanni Laterano, 4 Rome

Website:

www.vatican.va/various/basiliche/san_giovanni/index_it.htm

St. Mary Major (*Santa Maria Maggiore*)

The last of the four Major Basilicas in Rome is located on Esquiline Hill, the highest of the seven hills of Rome. Dedicated to St. Mary, the Greatest of the Saints, St. Mary Major has an interesting history. On August 5, each year, at the conclusion of the solemn mass, a shower of white rose petals falls from the dome of the Chapel of Our Lady. At sunset the same day, another staged "snowfall" is released in the square outside the basilica.

A detail of the triumphal arch in St. Mary Major's. (Courtesy of Bret Thoman)

These traditions are owed to the church's ancient name. Prior to 1960, the Feast of the Dedication of the Basilica of Saint Mary Major was known as the Dedication of St. Mary of the Snows. According to an ancient tradition, a Roman patrician named John prayed to the Blessed Mother so that she would show him how to bequeath his wealth. She appeared to him and said that she wished to have a church built in her honor. Regarding its location, she said that she would give a sign in snow. Indeed, on August 5, it snowed on Esquiline Hill. Anyone who has been to the Eternal City during the scorching summer heat will acknowledge this to be a miracle indeed.

With its coffered ceiling, Cosmatesque floors, mosaics, and brilliant decorations, St. Mary's feels like St. John's and St. Paul's. However, it is smaller, usually less crowded, and offers a more intimate feeling. As in the other basilicas, it features a number of important artifacts, relics, and artwork. The most significant relic is preserved beneath the high altar in the Crypt of the Nativity, also known as the Bethlehem Crypt. Within a crystal reliquary are three pieces of wood believed to be from Christ's manger in Bethlehem.

The most famous image in the church is a Byzantine icon known as "Salus Populi Romani" (Health, or Salvation, of the Roman People), conserved within the Borghese (Pauline) Chapel in the left transept. Above the icon is a beautiful golden relief depicting the story of the Snows. Pope Liberius can be seen delineating the boundaries of the church in the snow.

On the right transept is another beautifully decorated altar, which boasts a massive, ornate tabernacle. It is known colloquially as the Sistine Chapel because it was designed by Pope Sixtus, the same pontiff who designed the more famous Sistine Chapel in the Vatican. Another holy relic is the skull of St. Pancras, a fourteen-year-old orphan who converted to Christianity. After being brought to Rome by his uncle, St. Dionysius, he was martyred along with St. Nereus, St. Achilleus, and St. Domitilla around 304 A.D. for the crime of not renouncing Christianity.

Plan your visit:
Address: Piazza di Santa Maria Maggiore, Rome
Website: www.basilicasantamariamaggiore.va

Holy Cross in Jerusalem (*Santa Croce in Gerusalemme*)

After the four Major Basilicas, it is time to visit the three minor ones. The first is known as Holy Cross in Jerusalem. Located a short distance from St. John in Lateran, this church also dates to the early fourth century, at the time of Constantine. Though the nave of Santa Croce is not grandiose like the other basilicas, its floor, apse, and dome are exceedingly ornate. The main attraction is its impressive collection of relics, conserved in a room to the left of the main altar.

The "Titulus Crucis" relic kept at the Reliquary Chapel in Basilica of Santa Croce in Jerusalem by Babizhet (CC BY-SA 3.0)

It is believed that Empress Helena, the mother of Emperor Constantine, brought two significant relics to Rome from the Holy Land: pieces of wood believed to be from the True Cross and one of the nails used in the Crucifixion. Other relics added to the collection in later centuries include a reliquary containing fragments of the Grotto of the Nativity and the Holy Sepulchre, the index finger of St. Thomas, two thorns from the Crown of Jesus, and the *Titulus Crucis* (Title of the Cross), the wooden tablet placed atop the Cross, usually written as "INRI."
Plan your visit:

Address: Piazza di S. Croce in Gerusalemme, 10 Rome
Website: www.santacroceroma.it/en/

St. Lawrence outside the Walls (*San Lorenzo fuori le Mura*)

The next Minor Basilica on the Seven-Church route is St. Lawrence outside the Walls. St. Lawrence was a deacon charged with helping the poor and needy in the ancient Roman era. During the persecutions, he was ordered to turn over the riches of the Church to the empire. Instead, he called out the poor and announced that they were the "true treasure of the Church." As a result, he was ordered to be slowly burned alive on a gridiron. It is said that he jested with his tormentors, telling them to turn him over as he was "done on the first side." His martyrdom took place in 258 A.D. under the reign of Valerian.

The Basilica of St. Lawrence is beloved by local Romans. With its sunken entrance, covered portico, main nave, and two side aisles, it has an ancient feel to it. Once again, it was Emperor Constantine who, in 330, had a large cemetery church built near the tomb of St. Lawrence to house the remains of all those who wanted to be buried close to him. Later, in 580, Pope Pelagius II began construction on a new church and covered the apse with mosaics. (Only those in the arch remain.) At the beginning of the thirteenth century, Pope Honorius III completely rebuilt the Pelagian basilica. What remains today is an amalgamation of two churches.

The tomb of St. Lawrence and the gridiron on which he was martyred can be visited in the crypt beneath the nave. Relics believed to be those of St. Stephen, the first martyr, are also conserved here. Additionally, five popes are buried within: St. Zosimo, St. Sixtus III, St. Hilarius, Damasus II, and Bl. Pope Pius IX (the longest serving pope, after St. Peter).
Plan your visit:
Address: Piazzale del Verano, 3 Rome

St. Sebastian outside the Walls (*San Sebastiano fuori le Mura*)
The seventh and final church on the route is located just outside
the city walls along the Via Appia Antica: the Basilica of St.
Sebastian. Devotion to St. Sebastian, a Roman martyr, was
widespread in ancient times. According to hagiographical
legends, St. Sebastian was a Christian serving in the Roman
army. He was tied to a post and shot through with arrows during
the persecutions of Emperor Diocletian. Instead of dying, he
was rescued and healed by St. Irenaeus of Rome. Again,
according to tradition, after his recovery, he went to the
emperor to warn him about his sins. This time, he was clubbed
to death.

The original church was built in the fourth century (once again)
by Emperor Constantine. For a period of time, the remains of
Sts. Peter and Paul were kept here for safekeeping during the
persecutions. After they were returned to their original sites, the
church was dedicated to the Memory of the Apostles. When the
remains of St. Sebastian were deposited in the catacombs here,
the church took on the present name.

The interior consists of a single nave with an engraved wooden
ceiling. In keeping with its title as a Minor Basilica, it is
considerably smaller than the Major Basilicas. A statue of St.
Sebastian at the first side altar on the left greets pilgrims upon
entering. The Chapel of Relics houses one of the arrows that
was shot at St. Sebastian.
Plan your visit:
Website: www.sansebastianofuorilemura.org/

Sanctuary of Our Lady of Divine Love (*Santuario della
Madonna del Divino Amore*)
St. John Paul II removed the Church of St. Sebastian from the
"official" list of the seven churches for the Jubilee pilgrimage

route of 2000. In its place, he added the Sanctuary of Our Lady of Divine Love (*Santuario della Madonna di Divino Amore*), located south of Rome. The complex is made up of two churches, one begun in 1743 and the other in 1999. It is known for a miracle that took place in 1740, when a pilgrim was surrounded by dogs. He cried out to Our Lady, and the dogs left him alone.

Plan your visit:

Address: Via del Santuario, 10 Rome

Website: www.santuariodivinoamore.com

The European Itinerary

The *Iter Europaeum* (European Itinerary) is a pilgrim route that connects churches linked to the various countries of the European Union. It consists of twenty-eight churches or basilicas that are linked to a particular EU member state, based on artistic or cultural reasons or because the church has a tradition of welcoming pilgrims from that particular country. Visit this site for more information:

www.iubilaeum2025.va/en/pellegrinaggio/cammini-giubilari-dentro-roma/iter-europaeum.html

Patronesses of Europe and Women Doctors of the Church

This unique pilgrimage route connects churches associated with female saints—in particular, those who have been proclaimed Patronesses of Europe or Doctors of the Church. Of note are St. Bridget, St. Catherine of Siena, St. Teresa Benedicta of the Cross, St. Cecilia, St. Hildegard of Bingen, St. Thérèse of Lisieux (the Little Flower), and St. Teresa of Avila.

Visit this link for more information:

www.iubilaeum2025.va/en/pellegrinaggio/cammini-giubilari-dentro-roma/Donne-Patrone-Europa-e-Dottori-della-Chiesa.html

Via Appia and the Catacombs

The Via Appia Antica (Appian Way) is rich in history and spirituality. It is known for the famed catacombs as well as a number of significant early churches. Today, a protected archaeological site, the Via Appia is a delightful place to walk around or rent bikes.

Via Appia within the ancient city of Minturno. (Public Domain)

The Via Appia was an early Roman road built in 312 B.C. to connect Rome to southern Italy. Stretching 400 miles all the way from Rome to Brindisi, it was known as the Queen of the Roads. Today, the first ten miles of the Appian Way are protected as a state park (Parco dell'Appia Antica). Sections of it are remarkably well preserved, and it is an ideal area to get out and explore by bike or on foot. Though it is surrounded by urban Rome, it has the feel of a previous century. There are even flocks of sheep still grazing around the ancient Roman ruins.

The first church is not far from Rome's city walls. It is unique in that its name is a question: *Domine, quo vadis?* (Lord, where are you going?). This tiny, ninth-century church (renovated in the seventeenth century) was built on the spot where, according to a hagiographical tradition, St. Peter was fleeing the city to escape the persecutions of Emperor Nero. He reportedly had a vision of Christ, whom he asked, "Lord, where are you going?" Christ replied, "I am going to Rome to be crucified again." This gave Peter the faith and courage to return to Rome, where he met his martyrdom. Just inside the nave is a stone tablet on the floor with the alleged footprints of Jesus as he ascended to Heaven a second time.

The next stop is to the largest and most significant of the excavated catacombs in Rome: St. Callixtus (San Callisto). The word catacombs derives from Greek, *kata kumbas*, or Latin, *catacumbas*, which means "near the hollows"; that is, a sunken section along the Via Appia. In Roman times, burial within the city walls was prohibited, and burial grounds were all located outside the city walls. Tunnels and tombs were easily cut in the soft volcanic rock below ground, known as tuff, or *tufa* in Italian.

St. Callixtus is the name of the deacon who administered the cemetery, which served as the official cemetery for the Christian community during the ancient Roman persecutions. It is estimated that around 300,000 Christians were buried here, many of whom were martyrs. Most were interred in nondescript niches in the tunnels, while the wealthy had their own mausoleums. Several early popes were buried here, as was one of the most beloved Virgin Martyrs, St. Cecilia.

Devotion to the early martyrs was widespread in the ancient Church, and the faithful often came to the catacombs to pay homage to them, especially in late antiquity when Christianity became legal. During the barbarian invasions, the catacombs were sealed to protect them from looting. In time, they were abandoned and forgotten. In the seventeenth and eighteenth centuries, archaeologists discovered the catacombs and began excavating them. Soon after, tourists on the Grand Tour visited the catacombs by candlelight, and legends grew about Christians hiding in the tunnels to escape persecution. This is an urban legend. No Christians lived in the catacombs for significant periods of time.

Niches within the Catacombs of St. Callixtus (Courtesy of Bret Thoman)

The Catacombs of San Callisto offers English-speaking tours by priests or seminarians from the Salesian Order (who has charge of these catacombs) or trained archaeologists. A visit will reveal sections of the tomb-filled tunnels that stretch for miles and are several layers deep.

Plan your visit:
Address: Via Appia Antica, 110/126 Rome
Website: www.catacombesancallisto.it/en/index.php

Not far from San Callisto are other catacombs open to the public. The Catacombs of San Sebastiano, Santa Domitilla, and Santa Priscilla all offer guided tours.

Vatican City

Completely landlocked by Rome is Vatican City (La Città del Vaticano). Joyful pilgrims to the Vatican have dubbed it Catholic Disneyland, as it is the "happiest place on earth" for the faithful. Pilgrims can spend days here and still not take in all there is to see. Made up of just forty-nine hectares (121 acres) and a population of under 1,000 full-time residents, the tiny microstate holds the status of the smallest country in the world.

Due to a long and complicated history between the modern country of Italy and the Catholic Church, the Vatican was granted full autonomy from Italy in 1929 in what is known as the Lateran Treaty. Within this small enclave is the residence of the pope, the Vicar of Christ, and the headquarters of the Catholic Church, or the Holy See. Also known as the See of Peter, the pope (currently Pope Francis) governs Vatican City and exercises his office as bishop of Rome and authority over the wider Catholic Church.

Highlights include St. Peter's Basilica and crypt, a tour of the Scavi archaeological site, and the Vatican Museums and Gardens. (Note that St. Peter's Basilica is open to the public, while the Scavi, Vatican Museums, and Vatican Gardens tours all require an entrance ticket with advance purchase.) Website (official Vatican): www.vaticanstate.va

St. Peter's Basilica (*la Basilica di San Pietro*)

The Basilica of St. Peter (described above) is the most visited site within Vatican City and one of the most visited sites in Rome. There is no charge for entrance. Currently, there is a dedicated access route for pilgrims called *"Percorso Preghiera"* (Prayer Route), located on the right-hand side of the colonnade by the security metal detectors and indicated by special yellow signs.

The interior of St. Peter's Basilica. (Courtesy of Bret Thoman)

The Vatican Museums (*I Musei Vaticani*)

The Vatican Museums are the public museums of Vatican City. What began as the personal art collection of the popes in the Renaissance era was converted into a museum by Pope Julius II in the early sixteenth century. It was the first exhibit of its kind and is considered the first modern museum ever established.

The collection of artwork in the Vatican Museums is vast. Divided into twenty-four sections, it contains some 70,000 works, of which 20,000 are on display. Collections include ancient art and sculptures, bronze statues and mosaics, and a manicured courtyard. Highlights include the Pinacoteca (art gallery), Pio Clementino Museum (for sculpture), Egyptian Museum, Map Gallery, and spiral staircase. The main attractions are the Raphael rooms and the Sistine Chapel, where the tour concludes and is included in the ticket entrance. Tickets should be purchased in advance online. Website: m.museivaticani.va/content/museivaticani-mobile/en.html

The Scavi Tour (*Gli Scavi*)

A visit to the Scavi archaeological site is another highly sought-after experience. Here, visitors can explore the ancient necropolis and streets that were covered during the construction of the first basilica of St. Peter by order of Emperor Constantine. The highlight is a quick glimpse of the ancient red trophaeum (monument) built over St. Peter's tomb. Tour groups are organized by language. English-language tours are conducted by seminarians from the North American College, the prestigious American seminary in Rome, or trained archeologists.

The only way to book a tour is by contacting the Scavi office directly. It is recommended to do so well in advance, as only a maximum of 250 people per day are permitted (due to carbon dioxide limits) and slots fill up quickly. When you initiate contact, you are only making a request. Given the limited space, you should provide a range of available days and times you have available. Website: www.scavi.va/content/scavi/en.html

Papal Audience and Angelus

An audience with the pope is a special event. Each Wednesday morning, the pope reads from Scripture and gives a reflection in Italian and Spanish. Native speakers of other languages read the same verses and reflections in their languages. Tickets are required to access seats in the square. Up to a handful of tickets can be obtained by simply asking the Swiss Guards posted at the Petriano Gate (to the left of the façade of St. Peter's) at least one day prior to the audience. Otherwise, tickets for larger groups should be obtained by contacting the Prefect of the Pontifical Household and picked up at least one day in advance. There is no cost.
Website: www.vatican.va/various/prefettura/index_en.html

If you are not in Rome on Wednesday, Sundays are another option to see the pope. Each Sunday at noon, the pope gives a reflection in Italian, prays the Angelus in Latin, and grants an apostolic blessing in Latin. He appears from the second window in the Apostolic Palace, while a loudspeaker broadcasts the prayer and blessing. No tickets are required, and you can stand anywhere in the square to see him. (The Angelus depends on the Holy Father's physical presence in Rome.)

Other Pilgrimage Sites

Well-known Churches and Religious Sites:

The Pantheon (*Il Pantheon*): The Pantheon was built as a pagan temple around 25 B.C. by Agripa (the son-in-law of Emperor Augustus) and dedicated to all gods; hence, the etymological sense of the word (*pan-* [all] + *theos* [gods]). It is the best-preserved building from antiquity in Rome and perhaps the world. In 608 A.D., it was consecrated as a Christian church under Pope Boniface IV and consecrated to Mary and the Martyrs. Inside are the tombs of the kings of Italy and the tomb of Raphael, the great Renaissance painter. (Since 2023, the Pantheon requires a fee to enter.)

St. Mary over Minerva (*Santa Maria sopra Minerva*): Built on the foundations of a temple dedicated to Isis, this thirteenth-century Dominican church is situated next to the Pantheon. It is unique in that it is the only Gothic church in the city of Rome. Many pilgrims come here to pay homage to St. Catherine of Siena, a Dominican tertiary, whose body is preserved here (though her skull and finger are on display in the Dominican church in Siena). Of note in the interior is a work by Michelangelo, *Christ of Minerva*, sculpted in 1521. In the square in front of the church, there is a statue of an elephant and an obelisk by Bernini.

St. Clement at the Lateran (*San Clemente al Laterano*): This unique Minor Basilica is not far from St. John Lateran. Dedicated to Pope Clement I, it consists of a three-tiered complex of two churches (one from the twelfth century, the other from the fourth), both atop an ancient Roman home. (A fee is required to enter.)

The Colosseum (*Il Colosseo*): Though not a church, the renowned Colosseum is considered part of a pilgrimage itinerary, as many Christians were martyred here. It is also the site of the Way of the Cross, led by the pope each year on Good Friday. The Colosseum is the largest ancient amphitheater ever built and is the largest standing amphitheater in the world today. A thorough visit takes several hours and requires a museum entrance fee, which also includes entrance to the adjacent Roman Forum. Advance ticket purchases are required. Website: ticketing.colosseo.it/en/

The Colosseum in Rome. (Courtesy of Bret Thoman)

St. Peter in Chains (*San Pietro in Vincoli*): Not far from the Colosseum, this fifth-century church holds chains reputed to be those that bound St. Peter after his arrest. To the right is a famous statue of Moses, popularly known as the "Horned Moses," sculpted by Michelangelo for the tomb of Pope Julius II.

St. Louis of the French (*San Luigi dei Francesi*): Located next to the Italian Senate building, this sixteenth-century basilica was built to serve the French Catholic community. It boasts three paintings by Caravaggio, the master of the chiaroscuro technique, including his masterpiece, *The Calling of St. Matthew*.

The Calling of St. Matthew by Caravaggio. (Courtesy of Bret Thoman)

New Church (*Chiesa Nuova*); also known as Santa Maria in Vallicella: While this church features a beautiful Baroque interior with magnificent seventeenth-century paintings, many pilgrims come to pay homage to St. Philip Neri, founder of the Oratorians, a religious congregation of secular priests. From a well-to-do family in Florence, St. Philip Neri came to Rome in the sixteenth century and made a name for himself ministering to the poorest residents in the streets with a zestful personality. He is buried in the Blessed Sacrament chapel on the left

The tomb of St. Philip Neri. (Courtesy of Bret Thoman)

St. Andrew of Fratte (*Sant'Andrea delle Fratte*): Located between the Spanish Steps and Trevi Fountain, the Basilica of Sant'Andrea delle Fratte is one of the most beautiful churches in the entire city. For pilgrims, it is the site of a significant Marian apparition. On January 20, 1842, the Virgin Mary appeared to a Jewish man named Alphonse Ratisbonne, a young lawyer and banker fiercely hostile to the Catholic religion. Inside this church, he had a vision of Mary, converted to Catholicism, and eventually became a Jesuit priest. The chapel where the apparition took place was consecrated to the Blessed Virgin Mary with the title of Our Lady of the Medal. In fact, before the apparition and his conversion, Ratisbonne wore a Miraculous Medal, though he did so out of mockery.

Saints John and Paul on the Caelian Hill (*Santi Giovanni e Paolo al Celio*): The ancient basilica was built in 398 A.D. over the home of two Roman soldiers, John and Paul, martyred under Emperor Julian in 362. It is home to the Passionists and is the burial place of St. Paul of the Cross, founder of the Congregation of the Passionists.

Abbey of the Three Fountains (*Abbazia delle Tre Fontane*): The abbey is located three kilometers (2 mi) from the Basilica of St. Paul's outside the Walls. Though surrounded by urban Rome, the large complex, consisting of three churches and terrains, offers a peaceful respite from the hubbub of the city. Administered by Cistercian monks, it is known for raising the lambs, whose wool is used to weave the pallia of new archbishops. More important, it is believed that St. Paul was decapitated in an area now enclosed by the first church, known as the Church of St. Paul of the Fountains. When his head hit the ground, according to the legend, it bounced three times, leading to the emergence of water and the extant fountains. The second church is built over the relics of St. Zeno and his legionaries, while the third is dedicated to Sts. Vincent and Anastasius. Across from the abbey entrance is a grotto where a Marian apparition took place. In 1947, Our Lady appeared to Bruno Cornacchiola and his three children. Afterwards, he converted and rejoined the Catholic Church.

St. Mary in Trastevere (*Santa Maria in Trastevere*): Located in the popular Trastevere district, this is the oldest Marian church in Rome. After several renovations and restorations, the church has retained much of its medieval character, including golden mosaics.

St. Cecilia in Trastevere (*Santa Cecilia in Trastevere*): A short walk from Santa Maria is the famed, ninth-century Basilica of Santa

Cecilia in Trastevere. Built over the third-century home of St. Cecilia, the relics of the famed patroness of musicians are interred here. Originally buried in the Catacombs of San Callisto, in 821 her body was exhumed by Pope Paschal I and placed in this church, built purposefully for her. Her body rests within the crypt under the main altar. Below the main altar is a sculpture by Stefano Maderno of the saint's body as he saw it in the sixteenth century after she was exhumed. (A copy of the statue fills the niche in the Catacombs of San Callisto, where her body was originally buried.)

Basilica of St. Augustine (*Sant'Agostino*): The Basilica of St. Augustine, located in Campo Marzio (just northeast of Piazza Navona), is the Mother Church of the Augustinian Order. Originally built in 1286, the current basilica is from the Renaissance. While it houses artwork by Caravaggio, Raphael, and Guercino, many pilgrims come here to pay homage to St. Augustine's mother, St. Monica, whose tomb is here.

The Jesuit Church of Jesus (*Chiesa del Gesù*): In the center of Rome along the Corso (a few steps from the Largo di Torre Argentina, where Julius Caesar was assassinated), is the Mother Church of the Jesuit Order. Commonly known as Il Gesù, it is considered the archetype of post-counter-reformation Roman architecture. It conserves the tomb of the founder of the order, St. Ignatius of Loyola. St. Ignatius was from Loyola in the Basque region of Spain and led a military life before his conversion. While convalescing after a leg injury from battle, he read the lives of the saints, which led to his conversion. He went on to found the Society of Jesus, also known as the Jesuits, which took on an important role during the Counter-Reformation. He led the order from the headquarters next to this church, where he died on July 31, 1556. He is buried under the altar in the left transept. The church also houses an arm of St. Francis Xavier (missioner to the East) in a reliquary above the altar in the right transept and the remains of St. Peter Faber, an early companion of St. Ignatius. Inside the adjacent residence are four of the saint's rooms, which can be visited upon request.

Church of St. Ignatius of Loyola (*Sant'Ignazio di Loyola*): The other Jesuit church in Rome is dedicated to the founder, St. Ignatius of Loyola. Located in Campo Marzio between the Pantheon and Trevi Fountain, it was built in the seventeenth century as the chapel for the study house for the Jesuits, known as the Roman College. (The center was later moved and renamed the Pontifical Gregorian University.) The decorative style is from the baroque era. Of note are the unique ceiling frescos and a "false dome" by Andrea Pozzo.

Saint Sabina in Aventine (*Santa Sabina all'Aventino*): Located on Aventine Hill, this is the oldest basilica in Rome that has preserved its original plan and simplicity. Though St. Sabina was founded in 425, it was donated to St. Dominic of Guzman, founder of the Dominican Order, by Pope Honorius III in 1219. It is the Mother Church of the Order of Preachers (the Dominicans). St. Dominic's room can be visited.

St. Mary of the Conception of the Capuchins (*Santa Maria della Concezione dei Cappuccini*): The Capuchin "Bone Church," as it is known locally, is a popular visit in Rome. Its main attraction is the crypt that preserves five chapels adorned with the bones of more than 4,000 Capuchin friars buried here between 1500 and 1870. There are altars and murals made of bones, and even some intact skeletons clothed in Capuchin habits. Though the site may strike visitors as macabre, it is intended to be a *memento mori* (reminder of death). A plaque on the wall says (translated from Latin): "What you are now, we once were; what we are now, you shall be."

The Church of the Mamertine Prison (*La Chiesa del Carcere Mamertino*): Located along the Roman Forum, next to the huge monument dedicated to Victor Emanuel II, in the crypt is the ancient Mamertine prison. According to legend, this is the site where Sts. Peter and Paul were imprisoned.

St. Mary of the People (*Santa Maria del Popolo*): Located in the popular square Piazza del Popolo, this inconspicuous Renaissance-era church features an interior replete with art. Each of its seven chapels contains masterpieces by Renaissance and Baroque artists, including Pinturicchio, Raphael, Bernini, and Caravaggio.

St. Praxedes (*Santa Prassede*): From the Basilica of St. Mary Major, head to the nearby church dedicated to St. Prassede, the sister of St. Pudenziana. Within the chapel of San Zeno, immediately on the left, are some of the city's most beautiful Byzantine mosaics. To the right is a relic reputed to be the pillar on which Christ was scourged. According to tradition, St. Helena brought this back to Rome from the Holy Land.

St. Pudentiana (*Santa Pudenziana*): Some say this is Rome's oldest church, though the present church dates to the fourth century. It is dedicated to St. Pudentiana, sister of Praxedes and daughter of Pudens (mentioned by St. Paul in 2 Timothy 4:21). These two sisters are known for having wiped the blood of the martyrs after their execution. While the church is adorned with numerous Roman mosaics from the fourth century (especially in the apse), it is also known for a Eucharistic miracle that took place in the altar of the Caetani Chapel. To this day, the imprint of the Host and stain of Blood remain on a step after the Host fell from the hands of a priest who expressed doubt regarding the Real Presence of Christ in the sacrament of the Eucharist.

Lesser-known Churches

From the Middle Ages: San Marco at Capitol, Santa Agnese outside the Walls, Santi Cosmos and Damian, and Santa Maria in Cosmedin.

From the Renaissance era: Santa Maria della Pace, San Pietro in Montorio, Oratorio del Gonfalone, and San Giovanni dei Fiorentini.

From the Baroque era: San Carlino Quattro Fontane, Santa Maria della Vittoria, Sant'Ivo alla Sapienza, Sant'Andrea al Quirinale, Sant'Andrea della Valle, San Carlo ai Catinari, Sts. Carlo and Ambrogio al Corso, Santa Maria in Vallicella, Santi Apostoli, and Santa Maria in Campitelli.

Tourist Attractions

<u>Navona Square</u> (*Piazza Navona*): One of Rome's most charming squares, Piazza Navona is constantly buzzing with people, especially in the late evening when Romans go out. The oval shape is significant in that it was originally a stadium constructed by Emperor Domitian in 86 A.D. Throughout the Middle Ages, it continued to host games until they were banned. Today, it is the embodiment of Baroque Rome. The square features two fountains by rival Baroque masters, Bernini and Borromini. On one side of the square is a church containing the relics of St. Agnes of Rome—martyred during the persecutions—designed by Borromini for Pope Innocent X. In the center of the piazza is the Fontana dei Fiumi (Fountain of the Rivers), designed by Bernini and completed in 1651. It consists of an obelisk resting upon a rocky island populated by exotic animals and personifications of the four rivers in all known regions of the world at the time: the Nile, Ganges, Danube, and Rio de la Plata.

<u>Spanish Steps</u> (*Piazza di Spagna*): The name derives from the presence of the nearby Spanish. From the eighteenth century, it was a meeting place for foreigners—mainly the English—who came to Rome to visit the ruins of antiquity. (John Keats lived and died in the house to the right.) A large stairway connects the square with the Church of Trinità dei Monti. At the foot of the stairway is the Fontana della Barcaccia (Boat Fountain) by Pietro Bernini and his son Gianlorenzo from 1629.

<u>Trevi Fountain</u> (*Fontana di Trevi*): In the heart of Rome stands one of the most celebrated fountains in the world. At 26 meters (86 ft) high and 49 meters (161 ft) wide, it is the largest Baroque fountain in Rome. Its name derives from its location at the juncture of *tre vie* (three roads). Of note is the fact that it marks the terminating point of the water from an ancient Roman aqueduct (fourteen miles long) built in 19 B.C. to bring water

from a spring outside the city. After the Goths sacked Rome and destroyed the aqueducts in the sixth century, the Romans were forced to draw water from polluted wells and the Tiber. The Trevi aqueduct was rebuilt in the seventeenth century as the most ambitious of the Baroque fountains of Rome and completed in 1732 by Nicola Salvi. Following the ancient Roman custom of pilgrims who left coins on the tomb of St. Peter, it is believed that one's return to Rome is guaranteed by tossing a coin in the fountain. (A fee is now required to enter the Trevi Fountain area.)

Trevi Fountain. (Courtesy of Bret Thoman)

Visits near Rome

If you have some extra time during your stay in Rome, you may wish to head to the outskirts. Here are a few sites near Rome.

Ancient Ostia (Ostia Antica) Located at the end of the Via Ostiense, Ostia served as the port city in the era of ancient Rome. Over the centuries, the port filled with silt and solidified, creating the municipalities of modern Ostia, Isola Sacra, and Fiumicino, which are located between Ostia Antica and the actual sea. Today, much of the area has been excavated and is an archaeological site. Of interest to pilgrims is the fact that St. Monica, mother of St. Augustine, died here in 387 A.D. and was buried in the Church of Santa Aurea. In the sixth century, her body was transferred to the Basilica of St. Augustine in the center of Rome. A fragment of her original tomb can be seen in Sant'Aurea (near the entrance to the archaeological park).

Plan your visit:

Address: Viale dei Romagnoli, 717, 00119 Ostia Antica

Website: www.ostiaantica.beniculturali.it

Gandolfo Castle (Castel Gandolfo): Until the papacy of Pope Francis, popes used to summer at the papal residence in Castel Gandolfo. Though Pope Francis no longer utilizes it as such, it is still a popular visit. Located in the Roman Castles district near Lake Albano, it is lovely to visit, especially in the summer due to its cooler air. Located some twenty-five kilometers (16 mi) south of the Vatican, it holds extraterritorial status as one of the properties of the Holy See outside Italian jurisdiction. Today, the apostolic palace of Castel Gandolfo has been transformed into a museum. Tickets should be purchased on the Vatican Museum website (see above).

Plan your visit:

Address: Piazza della Libertà, 7, Rome

Getting Around

A good pair of walking shoes and fitness are essential for navigating Rome, as distances between sites can be vast. However, there are other options for getting around. An open-air hop-on/hop-off bus tour is an easy way to hit all the main sites. There are several companies offering bus tours, but perhaps the best for the pilgrim is the one operated by ORP (Opera Romana Pellegrinaggi), the Vatican Pilgrimage Office. The ORP route covers the most significant Christian sites and offers a headset with an English option that describes the sites as the bus passes by. As the name of the service implies, you can get on and off as many times as you like.

Rome is not car-friendly. The entire historic center is part of a Limited Traffic Zone (ZTL), and Roman traffic is notoriously chaotic. Public transportation in Rome is well-serviced. The subway (Metro) offers two lines, and the system is easy to navigate. City buses are inexpensive, too. However, it can be difficult to access the schedules and routes.

The most convenient way to get around Rome is via taxi. Although Roman cab drivers are notorious for gouging tourists, when they use the meter, taxis are not expensive. Make sure you get in the official white taxis and avoid the non-licensed ones. Note that taxis in Italy are not supposed to stop anywhere; that is, they cannot be hailed. Instead, passengers should line up at the official taxi stands, denoted by "TAXI" in black letters on an orange background.

Lastly, there is the option of using ride-sharing services. Uber and Lyft are available in Rome, though the most popular Roman ride-sharing app is Mytaxi

Important Websites

The Official Jubilee 2025 Website:
www.iubilaeum2025.va/en.html

The Major Basilicas of Rome:
www.vatican.va/various/basiliche/index_en.html

The Main Vatican Pilgrimage Website:
www.operaromanapellegrinaggi.org/en/pilgrimages/rome

A Secondary Vatican Pilgrimage Website:
www.annusfidei.va/content/novaevangelizatio/en/condividi/i
nfopointroma.html

The Diocese of Rome:
www.diocesidiroma.it

Accommodations with Religious Orders:
www.monasterystays.com

Tips on Traveling in Italy

ACCOMMODATIONS: Accommodations in Italy are comfortable, though there are cultural differences when compared to American and northern European hotels. Space is a luxury in Italy, and elevators, rooms, and bathrooms tend to be smaller and cramped. Given the high cost of energy in Europe, air conditioning and heating are used sparingly. Likewise, many hotels require inserting the key card into a wall slot to activate the lights. This ensures the lights will be turned off when no one is in the room.

VISITING CHURCHES: Churches in Italy are frequently closed for a variety of reasons. Typically (particularly in central and southern Italy), churches close for a few hours during the middle of the day. This is a custom in the Mediterranean world. Times vary, but the closing period typically begins around noon or 1:00 p.m. and ends in the early afternoon. Thus, a typical church might be open from 8:00 a.m. until 12:45 p.m., and then again from 3:30 until 7:00 p.m. Other times, churches may close indefinitely for renovations. Still other times, churches may be closed permanently because there is no one left to staff them. For planning purposes, it would be prudent to check the church's website in advance to verify it will be open when you plan on arriving.

ETIQUETTE: Appropriate dress is required in many churches and sanctuaries. Sleeveless shirts, short dresses, and short shorts are usually not permitted. Photographs are sometimes not allowed, either. Remember, churches are places of prayer, not museums. If there is a dress code or photography prohibition, it will be publicized on a sign at the entrance.

MEALS: Italy is renowned around the world for its culinary traditions. In fact, the Mediterranean diet has received the coveted designation Cultural Heritage of Humanity by UNESCO. However, people from northern Europe and North America sometimes find the meal times and amounts different from what they are accustomed to. Breakfast is continental. This means it is light, consisting often of cappuccino, a pastry, perhaps cereal, or toast and jam. Do not expect anything salty, like bacon and eggs. Lunch is the main meal of the day and begins (traditionally) at 1:00. It is served in courses. The *primo piatto*, or first dish, is almost always pasta. After the first dish comes the *secondo piatto*, or main course. The *secondo* consists of a meat like chicken, beef, or veal. The main course is always accompanied by a *contorno*, or side dish, like a vegetable or salad. A serving of fruit usually concludes the meal, unless (usually in formal settings) a real dessert is served. Dinner usually begins at 8:00 p.m. While most families have light dinners (consisting of leftovers from lunch, soup, or an omelet), hotels usually serve dinners according to the lunch experience described above.

WALKING: Visitors to Italy often comment that a lot of walking and stair climbing are required. While taxis and private or public transportation can reduce some of the distances, many city centers are closed to traffic, making walking necessary. If you are not used to walking, you should begin to do so before leaving.

WEATHER: Italy enjoys a pleasant Mediterranean climate. However, it is a large country with hundreds of miles of coastline, valleys and hills, and mountains, which makes for all kinds of microclimates. While the spring and fall seasons are usually delightful, winters are cold and sometimes rainy, and the summers are hot, sunny, and usually dry. Coastal areas in the south are tropical and mild, while inland regions are temperate and mountainous areas are cold. Visit the following Italian website for the most up-to-date weather forecasts: www.ilmeteo.it. (Click the British flag.)

PASSPORT: Citizens from EU countries, the United Kingdom, the United States, and Canada (and other countries) do not need a visa to enter Italy. However, one's passport must be valid for at least 90 days after the scheduled return date. Beginning in 2025, Schengen-area countries (including Italy) will require ETIAS travel authorization from all passengers coming from countries with visa waivers. The authorization is not a visa; it is a short application made on the ETIAS website with a small fee.

TIME ZONE: Italy has only one time zone, Central European Time (CET), which is GMT+1. Italy is six hours ahead of the Eastern Time

Zone in the United States. Thus, at 8:00 a.m. in New York, it is 2:00 p.m. in Italy. Italy observes daylight savings time, but according to a different calendar than in other countries. Thus, there are a few weeks each year when the time difference is nonstandard. Europeans use military times instead of a.m. or p.m. Thus, 2:00 p.m. would be written as 14:00.

CAUTION: Italy is generally safe, and violent crime is extremely rare. Nevertheless, many cities (especially Rome) are full of pickpockets and thieves. It is recommended to carry valuables in a hidden money belt or bag.

Books by Icona Press

The Complete Pilgrim Guide to Italy: Land of Saints and Sanctuaries, Miracles and Mystics. By Bret Thoman. 2024.

The Life of Padre Pio: Mystery, Miracles, and Mission. By Bret Thoman. 2024.

Following Padre Pio: A Journey of Discovery from Pietrelcina to San Giovanni Rotondo. By Bret Thoman. 2024. Second Edition.

Saint Francis of Assisi: Passion, Poverty and the Man Who Transformed the Church. TAN Books, 2016.

Saint Clare of Assisi: Light From the Cloister. TAN Books, 2017.

St. Maria Goretti: A Journey into Forgiveness and Redemption, by Bret Thoman. By Bret Thoman. 2021.

Following Maria Goretti: A Personal Journey from Her Birthplace to Martyrdom, by Bret Thoman. By Bret Thoman. 2024

"My Rosary": The Beloved Prayer of an Exorcist. Fr. Gabriele Amorth, translated by Bret Thoman. 2023.

About the Author

Born and raised in Atlanta, Georgia (USA), Bret Thoman currently lives in Loreto, Italy with his wife and three children. He has been a member of the Secular Franciscan Order (Third Order of St. Francis) since 2003. He has a master's degree in Italian from Middlebury College, a BA from the University of Georgia in foreign languages, and a certificate in Franciscan Studies. Bret is an FAA-licensed pilot and has logged over 3,500 hours of flight time.

His main activity is leading individuals and groups through Italy on pilgrimage for St. Francis Pilgrimages, the company he founded in 2004. www.stfrancispilgrimages.com.

He can be contacted at bret@stfrancispilgrimages.com.

All Bret's books are online at
www.amazon.com/Bret-Thoman/e/B0753K2PTJ.

Did this book help you in some way? If so, we'd love to hear about it. Sincere reviews on **Amazon** and **Goodreads** help readers find the right book they are looking for.

www.ingramcontent.com/pod-product-compliance
Lightning Source LLC
Chambersburg PA
CBHW060120050426
42448CB00010B/1968